Imagine you have a friend in Jakarta. She's spent her days and nights discovering the city's best experiences, sightseeing, dining and shopping. She leads you through the roads, along canals, down narrow *gangs*, sharing knowledge and making recommendations along the way.

Your guide, Janet Boileau, has published articles on Indonesian life and culture, business, travel and leisure in books and periodicals all over the world. She is the editor of several magazines, including *Jakarta Program*, the authoritative guide to what's on and where to go in the capital each month. She has also co-authored several documentaries and feature films on Indonesia.

Insight Pocket Guide: Jakarta is for the active traveller who wants the optimum pleasure from a brief visit to Jakarta. The author begins with an overview of Jakarta's development from a spice port to an emerging ASEAN capital, highlighting Indonesian history, culture, values and religion.

She then offers three full-day itineraries to familiarize you with Jakarta. The first begins with breakfast in the historic Hotel Indonesia, featured in the film *The Year of Living Dangerously*, takes in the primary city sights and ends with dinner in a curiosity shop left over from the Dutch colonial past.

These itineraries, which incorporate major places of interest like the National Monument and the old port of Sunda Kelapa, are followed by a selection of morning, afternoon and evening tours for you to combine as you please. Be it a tour of the city centre or a treasure hunt through alleyway antique shops, Janet Boileau's insights are always to the point. And, with a writer's curiosity, she knows Jakarta nightlife like the back of her hand.

Practical information on accommodations is in the What To Know section of the book. In order to make orientation and communication easier, Indonesian translations of important places and terms are included in the text and a brief language lesson can be found in the back of the book.

Jakarta has always been and still is an exotic and mysterious city. But the *Ibu Kota*, Mother City, of the Indonesians has entered the 1990s on the crest of a wave of development. Use this book as a catalyst, not an ironbound guide and, for the traveller with a sense of adventure, getting to know the new Jakarta is a fascinating, vibrant and colourful encounter.

Selamat Datang! Welcome!

Insight Pocket Guide:

JaKaRTa

First Edition

© **1991 APA Publications (HK) Ltd.**

All Rights Reserved

Printed in Singapore by

Höfer Press (Pte) Ltd

Fax: 65-861 6438

No part of this book
may be reproduced, stored in a
retrieval system or transmitted
in any form or means electronic,
mechanical, photocopying,
recording or otherwise,
without prior written permission
of *Apa Publications*.
Brief text quotations with use of
photographs are exempted for
book review purposes only.

INSIGHT POCKET GUIDES

Recommendations for a Short Stay

JaKarTa

Written by **Janet Boileau**
Directed by **Hans Höfer**
Design Concept by **V. Barl**
Art Direction by **Karen Hoisington**
Photography by **Ingo Jezierski**
Editorial Director **Michael Stachels**

Contents

Welcome 3
Introduction 10
History and Culture
    Landmarks 14
    Orang Betawi 15
    Culture 16
    Values 17
    Islam 18
    History 20

Day Itineraries
    Day 1: Getting Acquainted 22
    Day 2: Back In Old Batavia 28
    Day 3: Dragons In Paradise 32

Pick And Choose
A.M. Itineraries
    1. Fine Art 36
    2. Menteng Morning 38
    3. Indonesia In Miniature 40
    4. Bay Morning 42
    5. Antique Hunt 43
    6. Textile Tour 44

P.M. Itineraries
    1. Easy Afternoon 48
    2. Blok M 49
    3. To Market To Market 51
    4. Antiques And Tea 53

Nightlife
    1. Cultural Pursuits 54
    2. More Trivial Pursuits 55

Day Trips
1. Hill Safari **58**
2. Colonial Island Picnic **59**
3. Old Banten **60**
4. The Thousand Islands **61**
5. Carita Beach And Krakatau **62**
6. Pelabuhan Ratu **63**

Dining Experiences
A Taste Of Indonesia **64**
Street Food **65**
Dining Indonesian **66**
Dutch/Indonesian **67**
Other Cuisines **67**

Shopping
What To Buy **71**
Where To Buy It **76**

What To Know
1. Travel Essentials **78**
   When To Visit **78**
   Vaccinations And Health **78**
   Money Matters **78**
   Clothing **79**
   Electricity **79**
   Airport Tax **80**
2. Getting Acquainted **80**
   Geography **80**
   Climate **80**
   Time **80**
   How Not To Offend **80**
   Whom Do You Trust? **81**
   Tipping **81**
   Tourist Information **81**

3. Getting Around 82
    Limousines 82
    Taxis 82
    On Foot 82
    Local Vehicles 82
    Buses 83
    Rental Cars 83
    To And From The Airport 83
    Maps 83
4. Where To Stay 84
5. Business Hours 86
6. Public Holidays 95
7. Health And Emergencies 86
8. Communications And News 88
9. Museums 89
10. Sports Facilities 90
11. Special Information 90
    The Indonesian Language 90
12. Useful Addresses 93
13. Further Reading 98

Maps

    Western Indonesia 2
    Day 1: Getting Acquainted 23
    Day 3: Dragons In Paradise 33
    A.M. 1: Fine Art 36
    A.M. 2: Menteng Morning 38
    A.M. 6: Textile Tour 46
    P.M. 1: Easy Afternoon 48
    P.M. 3: To Market To Market **52/53**
    Jakarta 106

Dear Reader,

When I made my first acquaintance with Jakarta in 1974, the city was polluted, crowded, hot and stinking – a nasty but necessary gate one passed through as quickly as possible *en route* to the cultural heartlands of Java or the blissful beaches of Bali.

In 16 years things have changed. Bali has become a jetset playground and Jakarta an ASEAN capital, following fast on the heels of other Asian cities in terms of economic growth, urban development – and westernization. It is no longer the "big village" described in 10-year-old guide books but a sprawling metropolis spawning highrise office blocks, hotels and new businesses almost daily, with a civic administration desperately struggling to provide the services and amenities that will support a new city undergoing a constant and dynamic process of mutation.

Jakarta is not a city that renders its charms openly; the short stay visitor, unprepared, is probably the least likely to appreciate it. On a bad day it seems that nothing works, nobody understands anything and everything that can go wrong, will. It is not a figment of a travel weary imagination – Jakarta is a city in transition, with an over-burdened telephone system, a lumbering bureaucracy and some of the world's worst traffic jams. It is still polluted, crowded, hot and home to some memorable smells. But those of us who have made our homes here have learned to live with it. The secret to enjoying Jakarta lies not so much in WHAT to see but HOW to get round the traffic, when NOT to tackle the post office, where to walk, where to not even contemplate walking. Even when to sleep and when to get up. Enjoying Jakarta needs a touch of art.

Once you know how to approach it, Jakarta becomes a lively, light-hearted and very friendly town, full of little surprises, fascinating sights and spontaneous theatre. It is bemusing, confused and confusing, never how you expect it to be. It is rare to go from dawn to dusk without seeing something new or unusual, put together in a different way. It keeps you on your toes.

A very great part of what becomes endearing about Jakarta is its people – a polyglot mixture that encompasses the descendents of Portuguese sailors, Chinese traders, Indian slaves, Hindu kings, Vietnamese bronzesmiths, Dutch Protestants, Spanish Jesuits, British tea planters, Catholic missionaries, Muslim pilgrims, pearl divers, concubines, jungle warriors, drifters. Orang Betawi – the people of Jakarta, are irreverent, pious, patriotic, gifted improvisers and above all, survivors.

Jakarta in the 1990s is a boom town. It is changing very, very rapidly, chasing progress, becoming greener, cleaner and better organized. The promotion of tourism is a high priority and amenities for visitors are improving even as this book goes to press. But no matter how fast and far Indonesia reaches into the modern era, the capital city remains a bizarre and kaleidoscopic community; colourful, vigorous, industrious – and more than a little bit crazy. If being resident here has given me an enduring sense of Jakarta, it is that being a Jakartan means, and has always meant, living on the frontier.

HISTORY

Jakarta grew up around the ancient port of Sunda Kelapa at the mouth of the Ciliwung River. Since the 5th century, the date of the first records of Sunda Kelapa, vessels have called at the Javanese port, laden with rich spoils gathered along the eastern trading routes. The port was taken over by joint forces of the Muslim Javanese kingdoms of Banten and Demak in 1527 and given the name Jayakarta. It was to this town that Portuguese spice merchants came in the early 16th century and began the trading association with Europe that was to dictate the history of Jakarta, and Indonesia as a nation, for more than 400 years.

The Portuguese were followed into Indonesia by the Dutch. Under the leadership of an aggressive and determined envoy, Jan Pieterzoon Coen, the Dutch East India Company (VOC), proceeded forcibly to take possession of the town. They christened it Batavia.

Coen made Batavia the administrative and military capital of the VOC trading empire. As the city grew, administrative buildings and residential areas for the Dutch were removed from the industrial activities that formed the basis of the city's economy. Coen's successor Jacques Specx enlisted the help of Chinese traders in his building program, granting them the right to extract taxes for the use of the facilities they helped to construct. Under Specx, Batavia prospered

Culture

into the city that became known as the Queen of the East or Diamond City, named after the four towers of Coen's bastion which carried the names of precious stones.

The fortunes of Batavia waxed and waned with those of the VOC. While the Company's trading activities suffered from fluctuations in the international spice market, the cost of maintaining a military presence in the far-flung corners of the empire and from corruption within its own administration, the city too was beleaguered with problems. Buildings designed in the European style lacked adequate ventilation and their handsome façades deteriorated in the humid air. Pieterzoon Coen's elegant city of canals became a city of festering drains, a breeding ground for rats, malarial mosquitoes and epidemics of tropical disease.

The old city located in the Kota district had passed its prime and a new location was sought further south in the area that now surrounds the National Monument (Monas). Under Governor General Dandaels (1808-1818) a new city centre was developed, with tree-lined streets and handsome civic buildings in classic European architectural styles. Koningsplein, the Kings Square (now Medan Merdeka) became the fashionable hub of Batavia. A society playhouse was constructed alongside elegant shops; poorer working class inhabitants were shifted to outlying areas.

As Batavia entered the 20th century, a European city in the process of rapid modernization, a new class of Indonesians was emerging. With the benefit of Dutch education, young intellectuals were beginning to understand that the superiority of the European was not an innate quality but the result of cultural and historic influences.

In 1942 Japanese forces invaded Java, overcoming Dutch resistance with little difficulty and receiving a jubilant welcome from the Indonesian people. It quickly became apparent however that the Japanese occupation was just another form of oppression. Batavia, renamed Jakarta, became an occupied city with food shortages, outbreaks of violence and the destruction of many of the fine buildings left by the Europeans.

When Japan fell after Hiroshima, Indonesia was in no mood to return to colonial rule. In August 1945, at the urging of his compatriots, Sukarno declared Indonesia an independent republic.

Modern Jakarta owes much of its style to the period of nation building initiated by President Sukarno in the post war years. While his government struggled to find the means to effectively rule a nation that had been torn apart by war and left bereft of the infrastructure that had held it together since the days of J.P Coen, Sukarno built a capital city designed to embody the surging spirit of independence. He built highways, parks, extravagant buildings and monuments, creating a city that would be the public face of the nation and a concrete denial of the problems that beleaguered his country.

Political turmoil marred the final years of Sukarno's government. Military campaigns undertaken to quell unrest in various parts of the country strained the economy and inflation soared in the capital. In an horrific climax on 30 September 1965, during an attempted *coup*, six army generals were murdered and their bodies thrown into a disused well known as *Lubang Buaya* (the crocodile hole).

General Suharto, who succeeded Sukarno as President after the crisis of 1965, introduced the "New Order" government and a long-term program of reform. With a more pragmatic view of development, Suharto spearheaded the economic, bureaucratic and social revival of Jakarta, redefining its role as the capital of a developing nation and as a player in the ASEAN arena.

Present-day Jakarta reflects the development of the private sector economy. The business district centred around Jalan M.H.Thamrin has extended the full length of Jalan Sudirman and is now moving to encompass new areas in Kuningan, Kebayoran Baru and other purpose-built satellites. Office towers dominate the skyline, western-style shopping complexes, restaurants, entertainment venues and flashy housing estates are growing rapidly to cater for a newly affluent middle class.

Landmarks

Jakarta divides itself fairly easily into sightseeing blocks. The city follows a north-south axis, roughly equating its historical spread from the old harbour area in the north to the satellite suburbs in the south. One main arterial road runs the length of the city, which is one reason why there are such awful traffic jams. Various projects are under way to improve the road system and the traffic flow but the increase in number of cars continues to outstrip progress in this area and the roadworks help to disrupt traffic even further.

The official centre of the city is the National Monument, Monas, in Merdeka Square. With many government buildings in this area, Monas is the administrative heart of Jakarta; but for practical orientating purposes the hub is the Hotel Indonesia roundabout with the Welcome Monument at its centre. Many of the major hotels are situated on or near this roundabout and the main streets run north and south on Jl. Thamrin and Jl. Jendral Sudirman. Kebayoran Baru, a satellite suburb just south of the downtown area is a major shopping district. To the north of the Hotel Indonesia roundabout is Merdeka Square and Monas, further north is Chinatown and the historic area of the old port and early Dutch settlement.

Indispensable Jakarta landmarks, often quoted when giving directions, are the city's monuments, a legacy of the Sukarno era of fiery nationalism. Often referred to by irreverent nicknames such as "Pizza Man" or "Seven-Up", many of the statues adorn major intersections and can be a useful guide to remembering your way around.

Orang Betawi

Indonesia has absorbed people from throughout S.E. Asia and the Asian mainland, the Pacific and Europe. Many of these people entered through the great trading city that was called Jayakarta, Batavia and then Jakarta. Also congregating in the city from ancient times have been migrants from the regions of Indonesia – Sumatrans, Javanese, Minangkabau, Timorese, Balinese and so on. There are more than 300 distinct dialects spoken within Indonesia and as many ethnic groups to speak them. In Jakarta all these people mix.

The result is *orang betawi* (the Batavian). Jakartans speak their own dialect and have developed their own way of surviving in the great polyglot city that has become their home. Migrants continue to flood into Jakarta, many of them finding work in the "unofficial sector" as vendors, street sweepers, servants, professional scavengers. Many people also live on the street, cooking, washing, sleeping and earning a living as the world goes past around them.

The more well-to-do Jakartan still lives according to village traditions. Housewives go to market in the early morning to hunt out the freshest vegetables and stop in the street to gossip. Men in checkered or striped sarongs sit on benches watching the world go by and smoking *kretek*, the clove perfumed cigarette that lends its exotic scent to the air of the city. Others huddle in a group, absorbed by a roadside game of chess. Wherever you go in Jakarta, at whatever hour, people are busy. Even at three in the morning you may come across a little group sitting round a makeshift bonfire on the sidewalk, strumming guitars and singing softly while children play at their feet.

In recent years a new type of Jakartan has emerged. These are the entrepreneurs who have grown wealthy as the private business economy has flourished. Driving expensively taxed, imported cars and living in marble mansions in newly created garden suburbs, the *nouveau riche* have also created a new market for consumer items, imported luxury goods and the many outer trappings of western civilization.

Culture

Indonesian society has been washed by waves of cultural influence throughout the centuries. Ancient traditions and vestiges of a European colonial past live on, adapting to modern ways but never giving way completely. The ability to absorb, adapt and permute is one of the strengths of the Indonesian culture.

Visually there is little to remind the visitor of the past in Jakarta city itself. In the fervour of nationalism that followed independence, much of the beautiful colonial architecture was destroyed and only a handful of really old buildings remain. Traditional Indonesian architecture, seen mostly in the provinces, makes particularly fine use of sophisticated wood carving techniques. Decorative carved panels and doors from Jepara, Demak and Kudus in Java and Palembang in Sumatra appear as architectural ornaments and are as intricate and distinctly Indonesian as the elaborate *batik* cloth.

The textile arts are highly refined with widely differing techniques practised in the country's 27 different provinces. Cloth is both practical and ceremonial, decorative and utilitarian. In most regions other than Bali, textile arts are more highly developed and take the place of painting. A recent revival of interest in traditional textiles, spurred to a large degree by the fashion industry, has resulted in the reappearance of a wide range of excellent quality textiles, varying widely in texture, colour and motif but nearly always using natural fibres. Commercial dyes are now more commonly used, creating a brighter, more modern type of fabric alongside the more sombre cloths made with traditional vegetable dyes.

The geographic isolation of many of the islands and regions of Indonesia has produced a wide range of artisanic traditions and handcrafts. Wood and stone carving, metalsmithing and basketweaving are all highly developed. Decorative motifs reflect the influence of Hindu, Buddhist, classical Javanese, Islamic and European cultures. The most sacred craft object is the *kris*, a wavy-bladed dagger made from beaten layers of iron and steel with a decorated wood or ivory hilt and scabbard. Traditionally passed down between males from one generation to the next, the *kris* is a weapon, a talisman and a symbol of status, believed to possess magical powers.

The performing arts are for the most part, highly stylized. Traditional theatre, or *wayang*, is based on stories from the Hindu

Ramayana and *Mahabarata* epics, combined with and adapted to themes from traditional Javanese folklore. Wayang may be performed by humans (*wayang orang*), puppets (*wayang golek*) or shadow puppets (*wayang kulit*). The *wayang* contains an all-pervasive philosophy which colours and to a great extent still determines the Indonesian world view. Dance too, has its basis in legend. The Javanese tradition of court dancing, classical, formal, elaborately costumed and highly refined, continues with very little modern influence. Elsewhere in the archipelago, regional dancing is varied, colourful and more exuberant, often with much foot stomping and beating of drums.

The music of Java is the *gamelan*, played on a series of bronze gongs with the addition of drums, flute, a two stringed violin-type instrument, and perhaps zithers and a xylophone. The sound of the *gamelan*, once heard, becomes a memory of Indonesia that has a very particular, haunting quality. Pre-dating the *gamelan* is the *angklung*, an instrument composed of hollow bamboo chimes which are rattled. According to legend, the *angklung* was originally used to scare away birds in the rice paddies; the sound is light and pretty, evocative of sunshine, green fields and running water.

Values

Pancasila, the state ideology which underlies all political, social, economic and religious policies within Indonesia, is an essentially simple set of tenets espousing belief in god, national unity, democracy, humanitarianism and social justice. While *Pancasila* clearly defines the responsibilities and attitudes of society as a whole and the tenets of Islam dictate the behavioural guidelines for the majority of the population, at the heart of the Indonesian value system is *adat*, the codes and customs developed by tribal societies, progressively modified and reformed in response to outside influences including those of Hinduism, Buddhism, Islam and Christianity. Of these, the most pervasive and enduring was and is that of the ancient Javanese court culture and the philosophy of the *wayang*.

The Indonesian people are extremely courteous, highly conscious of status and the social graces that status requires. At the same time they are bound together by a sense of communal belonging so strong that the concept of "self" existing outside of a societal context, is alien and frowned upon. The immediate and extended family are all important, the opinions of all are taken into consideration when any important decisions are made. Respect of and obedience to authority developed in a paternalistic tribal past and compounded by several hundred years of patronistic colonialism, are deeply imbedded in the Indonesian psyche.

Discussion is a major feature of Indonesian life. At a national, communal and family level, decisions are made by a process of discussion leading to consensus; in daily life the process manifests as endless discussions of even minor details and as what appears to the visitor to be an abiding interest in other people's business. It is not intended as nosy or interfering when an Indonesian asks you where you are going or what you ate for lunch. A positive aspect of this group mentality is *gotong royong*, the policy of mutual assistance by which the individual receives support and a feeling of security within his family group and his community.

Islam

Mohammed, the prophet of Islam, was born in 571 AD and began teaching in 612. His proclaimed mission was to interpret the word of God. The Will of Allah, as revealed by Mohammed, was recorded in the Koran, the holy book of Islam compiled shortly after Mohammed's death.

At the heart of Islamic law are the Five Pillars or rituals: declaration of belief in Allah; praying five times daily; fasting during Ramadhan month; alms giving and the pilgrimage to Mecca.

Islam is a religion which permeates every aspect of social and personal life. The Will of Allah is supreme, the Koran contains dictates which cover behavioural codes for almost every situation as well as wisdom of a more profound nature. According to Islam, every man must account for his earthly deeds and his belief in Allah as the one and only God is a prerequisite for entry into heaven. The pilgrimage to Mecca, the most holy city of Islam, centres around a visit to the Kaaba, a sacred black stone which must be circled 7 times. A person who has completed the pilgrimage or *Haj*, receives the title *Haji* and may wear a white skull cap.

Islam was brought to Indonesia by merchants from the Gujarat region of India, around the 13th century. Orthodox, Arabian Islam followed some 500 years later after the Suez Canal was opened. Islam is now a fundament of the Indonesian way of life with a profound influence on art, law, education, society and custom. The call to prayer, intoned from mosque minarets, is part of the background noise of Jakarta, waking the city before dawn and punctuating the passing of the hours until the final call at dusk.

Right, the Monas Monument

HISTORY

5th century: Portuguese explorers arrive at Sunda Kelapa, already established as a trading port of the Hindu-Buddhist Kingdom of Sunda. The Portuguese sign a treaty with Sunda and are allowed to erect a warehouse.

1527: Sunda Kelapa is conquered by Fatahillah, a Muslim prince from the Kingdom of Demak in Central Java. He names his city Jayakarta.

1610: Dutch traders, already shipping spices from the Moluccas in the eastern part of the archipelago, gain permission to establish a warehouse in Jayakarta. A British "godown" follows.

1619: The Dutch East India Company (VOC), led by Jan Pieterzoon Coen, takes control of Jayakarta by force. Coen builds the city of Batavia, the hub of the powerful and acquisitive Dutch trading empire.

1700: After repelling several attacks by troops of the neighbouring kingdoms of Mataram and Banten, Batavia's power is consolidated, its influence extending over most of Java and beyond to other islands. The VOC trading empire is at its peak, the city of Batavia has become the elegant "Amsterdam of the East" with mansions, tree-lined boulevards, wide canals.

1740: Fears about the growing Chinese population in Batavia trigger government imposed restrictions. Unrest becomes a massacre as Chinatown is razed and thousands of Chinese citizens are slaughtered. Poor sanitation and disease claim other lives. The VOC begins to flounder under the burden of administrating the empire and growing bureaucratic corruption.

1799: The Government of the Netherlands, controlled by the French since their victory in the Napoleonic Wars four years earlier, dissolves the VOC. Herman William Dandaels is appointed Governor General of Batavia, leading the new colonial administration.

1811: Napoleon takes control of the Netherlands. Batavia becomes a French city, albeit briefly. In the same year Thomas Stamford Raffles, heading a British force out of Malacca, invades and takes over Batavia, instituting reforms and a progressive new administration.

1816: The Dutch regain the Netherlands and oust Raffles from Batavia. Batavia expands again as a refined Dutch colonial outpost.

1908: Indonesian students form Budi Utomo, the first nationalistic organization. Dissatisfaction with years of Dutch exploitation begins to foment throughout the country.

1926: The new Indonesian Communist Party instigates a revolt in Batavia and is crushed by the Dutch government. The following year, a student named Sukarno forms PNI (Patai Nasional Indonesia), a political movement with the goal towards Indonesian independence.

1927-1940: PNI membership and Sukarno's influence grow. The fiery nationalist is arrested twice by the Dutch and exiled. PNI is dissolved. The Dutch government initiates moves towards joint Dutch/Indonesian government.

1942: Japanese invade Batavia and the East Indies. The city is liberated from Dutch rule and renamed Jakarta.

1945: With Japanese defeat imminent, Indonesia attempts to declare independence before the Dutch return. Sukarno reads the Declaration of Independence and is made President of the new nation. The Dutch refuse to acknowledge the existence of his government.

1949: Under international pressure, the Netherlands government agrees to concede defeat. Sukarno moves his revolutionary government from Jogjakarta and raises the Indonesian flag outside the Merdeka Palace in Jakarta.

1950-1965: Under President Sukarno Indonesia struggles through troubled years of nation building. Jakarta is established as an Asian capital but grandiose physical development cannot disguise problems of soaring inflation, overcrowding and social unrest.

1965: Six army generals are kidnapped and murdered in an attempted *coup d'etat* subsequently attributed to the communist party. General Suharto, Chief of the Army strategic Reserve Command (KOSTRAD), takes control of the army and then the government.

1967: Sukarno is officially removed as head of state and placed under house arrest. Suharto is appointed President and inaugurates the New Order government.

1968 to Present: Suharto rebuilds the economy with guidance from American-trained experts. Oil boom revenues boost development, based on Repelita, a series of five-year plans. Suharto achieves rice self-sufficiency for the nation. When the world oil crisis of the late seventies threatens to pull the plug on development, the economy is deftly restructured and progress continues on the strength of non-oil exports, tourism and a newly revitalised capital market.

Day Itinераries

Sightseeing in Jakarta can be fascinating and enjoyable, or exhausting and frustrating. The best possible advice for the first time visitor is to TAKE IT EASY. Rushing around in the heat, battling against the traffic and trying to see and do everything, is a recipe for disaster. The following itineraries cover all the major tourist sites and a sampling of places and things that give Jakarta its own particular atmosphere. They are designed to show you around at a reasonable, life-preserving pace. The "Art of the Tropical Nap" is included for very good reasons.

Day 1

Getting Acquainted

Breakfast in an aviary; relics of Java man; bird's eye orientation from the top of the National Monument; lunch Sunda-style; Asia's biggest mosque; handicrafts from around the archipelago; the art of the tropical nap; sights & smells on Jl. Sabang; dinner in an old curiosity shop; angklung band.

Arjuna Statue

Day one in Jakarta kicks off at 9 a.m. from the **Hotel Indonesia**, Jakarta's first western-style hotel and most useful orientation point. Have breakfast in the **Ramayana Terrace**, a vast and somewhat bizarre coffee shop with a stained glass atrium, aviary (real and stuffed birds!) and mosaic wall mural reminiscent of the monumentalist period of the late President Sukarno. Try the favourite breakfast dish, *bubur ayam*, mild chicken porridge with egg and delicious savoury garnishes. Follow up with a good strong cup of *Java*; Indonesia is a coffee drinker's paradise. After breakfast step outside the lobby and observe the **Welcome Monument**, standing in a pool in the centre of the roundabout. Basically, the city runs north and south of this monument along two major thoroughfares, Jl.. M.H. Thamrin and Jl. Jend. Sudirman.

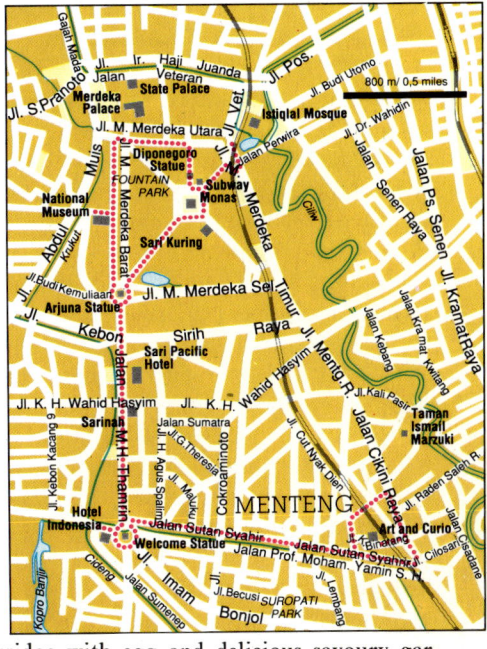

From the Hotel Indonesia walk clockwise round the roundabout and take the second street, Jl. M.H. Thamrin. On the left corner you will see Plaza Indonesia, a big hotel and shopping complex worth a visit during your stay. Walk three blocks along Jl. Thamrin. At the first major intersection (Jl. Wahid Hasyim), across the road on your right you will see Sarinah department store. You will be returning to it later. Continue on two more blocks to Jl. Budi Kemulyaan, cross over it and continue up Jl. Thamrin which at the next intersection becomes Jl. Medan Merdeka Barat. On your right, in the middle of the road, you will see the statue of **Arjuna**, hero of the Hindu *Mahabarata* epic, his chariot drawn by prancing horses. Due to its cheesy colour this statue is also rumoured to be the one that got away from a hotel butter carver.

National Museum

A short distance along Jl. Medan Merdeka Barat, on your left, you will come across a classic-looking building with columns and a statue of an elephant standing in front. The elephant was presented by King Chulalongkorn of Thailand in 1871.

This building is the **National Museum** (closed Monday). The **Ganesha society** gives guided tours in different languages on different days of the week. If there's one in your native tongue, tag along, if not, it's not a big museum so you can wander around on your own. Don't miss the treasure room on the second floor, the outstanding ceramics collection and the skull of the Java Man.

When you've had your fill of the museum, check the museum shop (near the main door), which offers some interesting souvenirs. Then cross the road and continue along Jl. Medan Merdeka Barat.

The park on your right is **Medan Merdeka**, originally the fashionable Konigsplein (Kings square) that formed the centre of 19th-century Batavia. Later, it was the site of mass gatherings which heralded the end of the Sukarno era amid conflict, violence and rhetoric. The centrepiece of Merdeka Square, an obelisk with a gold flame on top, is the **National Monument**, (MONAS), Sukarno's testament to the spirit of the Indonesian people.

At the end of Jl. Medan Merdeka Barat turn right into Jl. Medan Merdeka Utara. Across the road is the **Istana Negara**, or State Palace, built in 1879 as the official residence of the Dutch governors of Batavia. The palace is now the official residence of President Suharto and is not open to the public. With your back to the palace walk through the park, heading for the big bronze equine statue. This is **Diponegoro**, a Javanese warrior prince who led a fierce rebellion against the colonial Dutch. Near the base of Diponegoro is a subway which leads to the National Monument.

The Monas Monument, Sukarno's tribute to the Indonesians

Take the subway and you will emerge at the base of MONAS. Take a look at the dioramas depicting Indonesia's history, from prehistoric times until the present, and the meditation room before taking the elevator up to the tip of the monument for an unparalleled view of Jakarta.

The large dome visible across the road to the right of the entrance subway is that of the **Istiqlal Mosque**, the largest mosque in Southeast Asia. From this vantage point (unless it is a Sunday) you will also be able to study Jakarta's infamous traffic problems.

Come down from MONAS, walk back to back to Jl. Medan Merdaka Utara, turn right and continue on until you cross the road to visit the mosque. Afterwards, cross back to the park and continue clockwise round the park to **Sari Kuring**, a large, two-storey restaurant serving West Java (Sunda) cuisine and decorated in traditional Sundanese style with fountains, indoor gardens and fish pools. The speciality of Sundanese restaurants is baked fish (*ikan bakar*), caught fresh from the pool. Order a supremely refreshing *Es Kelapa Muda* (iced young coconut juice) while you wait for your fish to be cooked.

After lunch, hail a passing taxi (not yellow) outside the restaurant and take a short ride back to **Sarinah** department store. (If your first morning in Jakarta has already worn you out, save Sarinah for another day and proceed directly to the Tropical Nap.)

In Sarinah (named after President Sukarno's nursemaid), take the

escalator to the third floor and browse through a spectacular collection of handicrafts from throughout the 27 provinces of the Indonesian archipelago. Sarinah's prices are fixed (no bargaining necessary) and very reasonable. (Tips on what to buy are in the "Shopping" section of this book.) The next floor up is the *batik* floor, with everything from cheap but excellent blocked *batik* table cloths, to hand drawn *batik tulis* shirts and evening gowns in fine silk. Buy a colourful, flower-patterned cotton sarong from the large selection laid out in rows near the down escalator.

Before you leave Sarinah, pop down to the basement for pokerwork bamboo canisters packed with Toraja coffee (on the right by the supermarket checkout). Back upstairs, on the way out, stop at the wrapping station beneath the up escalator and buy a few sheets of cheap but unique batik gift wrap, or better still, for a couple of hundred rupiah (a few cents) have your gifts wrapped on the spot.

Laden with packages and foot sore, take a taxi back to your hotel to learn the most essential Art of the Tropical Nap. Take a cold shower, put on your *sarong*, drink a large glass of cold water and adopt the horizontal with your feet on the pillow instead of your head. Place a damp face cloth over your eyes. Snooze.

We re-emerge at 6 p.m. when the temperature has dropped, the traffic has thinned and the magic of the tropical evening is abroad. Take a taxi to the section of Jl. Agus Salim which is still universally known by its old name, **Jl. Sabang**. Start from the corner behind the Djakarta Theatre building, turn left and walk one block along Jl. Sabang which at this time of evening is lined with vendors' carts (mobile kitchens) producing a wonderful array of aromas and curious edibles such as fried bean curd balls stuffed with bean sprouts, fermented soy bean cakes (*tempe*) with small green chillies, and of course, Indonesia's incomparable answer to the *shish kebab* – *sate*.

You will pass tape shops with music blaring, tailor shops where you can have clothes professionally made to measure in a matter of days and Padang restaurants with their trademark window display of dishes piled into a pyramid. On Jl. Sabang you will also find cheap roadside shoe repairs, stores selling all kinds of small electrical miscellanies, stationery, strange grocery items, bath towels printed like dollar bills, "beware of the dog" signs and much much more. Wander along with your eyes tuned to small details. Exercise your nostrils. (As Jl. Sabang sidewalks are narrow and can be crowded, don't forget to keep your hand on your wallet or handbag.)

When you get to the end of Jl. Sabang (at the intersection with Jl. Kebon Sirih), cross over and walk back down the other side. Hail a passing cab or hop into an orange *bajaj* and head for **Taman Ismail Marzuki** (commonly called TIM), a few minutes away on Jl. Cikini Raya in Menteng. This is the centre of the performing arts in Jakarta and where you may catch a cultural performance during your stay (see daily listing in the *Jakarta Post*). Now that you know where TIM is, cross over the main road and head down Jl. Cikini II, a narrow street with a bakery on the corner. This small street runs down to the railway lines and turns sharp right to become Jl. Kebun Binatang.

As soon as you meet the railway tracks, turn the corner and you will see a sign, **"Art & Curio"**, a short way down on the right. Visit the garage shop on the way in for an odd collection of junk, antiques and memorabilia. The restaurant is dimly lit, atmospheric and staffed by waiters wearing the black felt *peci* hat which was worn during the Sukarno era as a symbol of nationalism. The food at Art & Curio is a mixture of Indonesian and Dutch/Continental. Try the *bitteballen* with pre-dinner drinks from the bar, then take your choice from the reasonably priced menu. The chicken salad is good. Your table may shake from time to time as the odd train thunders past through the night.

After dinner, work off a little of your surfeit with a short walk back up to Jl. Cikini Raya to flag down a taxi. Head for the **Sari Pacific** hotel, only a few minutes away. You will see a cascade of lights glittering in the lobby as you sweep up the steep driveway. The door will be opened by a bellhop in an ice cream vendor's suit, admitting you to a bright, pleasant lobby hung with trailing plants and Balinese paintings of flowers and birds. Turn to your left to reach the Melati Lounge where Jakarta's night owls gather for jazz and a nightcap. The hotel is proud of its imported jazz bands, but the real attraction is the resident group which, during the breaks, plays funky tunes on traditional instruments, including the extraordinary bamboo *angklung*.

Sculpture at the TIM

Back in Old Batavia

Buffet breakfast; wooden schooners in Sunda Kelapa; the old port; Taman Fatahillah; Blue Ocean lunch; antique market on Jl. Surabaya; an elegant cocktail; dinner colonial style.

To avoid the traffic between downtown and the old port in north Jakarta, an early start is essential unless your Day 2 happens to be a Sunday. Fortify yourself for a full morning with a 6.30 breakfast buffet at the **Marco Polo** hotel on Jl. Cikditiro in Menteng, not the most glamorous venue but open early and certainly one of the best value all-you-can eat spreads in town. Buy a packet of cologne wipes and a bottle of Aqua from the hotel shop and take an air-conditioned taxi for the ride to **Sunda Kelapa**, the old trading port of Batavia, in use since the 12th century.

Get out of the taxi at the entrance to Sunda Kelapa and pay a small fee to the guard in the toll booth. Walk along the wharf for a fascinating view of one of the world's last remaining commercial sailing fleets, the wooden *pinisi* schooners built by the seafaring Bugis people of South Sulawesi. With prows pointing skyward and stevedores unloading timber and other cargo down narrow plank gangways, the *pinisi* fleet is one of the most enthralling sights Jakarta has to offer, full of romance, history and salty adventure. Be wary of offers of "French" perfume and watches supposedly smuggled from abroad; mostly they are locally produced fakes.

Walk to the end of the wharf and then retrace your steps to the entrance gate. From there walk down the street to the bridge and turn right into Jl. Pakin. A few steps further on you will come to Jl. Pasar Ikan. **Pasar Ikan** (fish market) occupies what is left of the port area which served Portuguese and later Dutch traders who made their fortunes in the spice islands empire. On the right as you turn into Pasar Ikan is the **Uitkijk Tower**, built in 1839 as a lookout on the earlier Culemborg bastion. Of the 15 bastions that made up the original Batavia fortress, the four principals were lozenge-shaped and named after precious stones, earning

Sunda Kelapa, 12th century-old trading port

Batavia the nickname Diamond City. The tower was closed for repairs in 1989, reopening date unspecified.

Looking across Jl. Pakin from the tower you will see a long two-storeyed building which is what remains of the **VOC Shipyards**. The 18th-century Company Wharf was closed in 1809 due to insanitary conditions but the dilapidated yard and handsome building are still in use today.

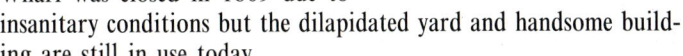
Uitkijk Tower, sentry to Culemborg

From the Uitkijk tower walk round into Jl. Pasar Ikan. On the left side of the street is the **Museum Bahari**, (Maritime Museum), originally built in 1652 as part of a warehouse complex in which the Dutch stored their trading spoils: pepper, cloves, nutmeg, coffee, tea, copper, tin, bales of cloth. Wander through the musty and atmospheric museum for a real sense of Batavia's past. On the second floor you can step out onto the only remaining section of the old **City Wall** that surrounded 17th-century Batavia.

When you emerge from the museum, cross the road and walk on down through the *pasar*, poking around in the shops crammed with seashells, ships chandlery, kitchen ware, fishing nets, stuffed turtles, ships and shoes and sealing wax. Follow the street round to the end where the fish market will be on your left, inside a concrete building. The smell will lead you to it. Take a look in if your nose can stand it, otherwise retrace your steps to the Uitkijk.

Hail a passing taxi and take a short drive to **Taman Fatahillah**,

Museum Bahari, musty 17th-century godown

the city square of old Batavia, planned by Governor General Jan Pieterzoon Coen in 1620. This plaza and the historic buildings which surround it are the subject of the first large scale conservation and restoration program undertaken by the present Jakarta administration. The large white building facing the square is the former **Stadhuis**, or city hall, which was the hub from which the fortunes of the Netherlands East Indies trading empire were controlled. The building now houses the **Jakarta History Museum** (closed Monday) with maps, porcelain, antiques and memorabilia from the Dutch period.

Wander around the Stadhuis then cross Jl. Pintu Utara on your left, to the **Wayang Museum**, also an historic building which contains a huge collection of puppets from throughout Indonesia and paraphernalia used in the wayang performance. There is also a memorial court in the museum, dedicated to Jan Pieterzoon Coen and other important figures from Batavia's distant past.

While sight-seeing around Taman Fatahillah, take a refreshment break at the dilapidated but curious **Restaurant Fatahillah and Art Shop.** Then proceed to the side of the square opposite the Wayang Museum. On the way inspect **Si Jagur**, a bronze Portuguese cannon brought to Batavia in 1641 after the defeat of Malacca. The cannon, which has a large fist molded on the butt end, was revered for a long time by the Javanese as a fertility god.

Restaurant Fatahillah

The impressive building set back from the road on the eastern side of the square is the **Fine Art Museum**, housed in the former Hall of Justice which was built in 1870. Inside is a superb collection of rare porcelain put together by Indonesia's former Vice-President, Adam Malik, plus paintings by well-known Indonesian artists.

After a long, footslogging morning you will be hot and hungry. Take a taxi from Taman Fatahillah down Jl. Hayam Wuruk to the **Hong Kong Bank building,** Wisma Hayam Wuruk, at number 8. On the third floor is **Siam Garden**, serving some of the best Thai food in Jakarta. A speciality of the house is iced coffee but ask for sugar syrup on the side if you don't like it too sweet. While you are waiting for your order, borrow the telephone and call **Oasis restaurant** (Tel: 321-355) to reserve your table for dinner.

After lunch take a taxi to **Jl. Surabaya**, Jakarta's famous antique flea market. Walk the length of Jl. Surabaya and bargain for your very own piece of old Batavia – brass lamps and candlesticks, plates, tea urns, stone jars, old *batiks*, trading beads, even brass beds and elaborately carved teak dressers. Clever fakes are generously mixed in with the real thing; buy what you like and don't pay big prices for anything unless you have an expert with you.

Anyone who does not need a Tropical Nap at this point must fall into the Hardened Traveller category. More laid-back types should head for their lodgings and rest up for the evening's activities.

A little extra sprucing up is required for our visit to **Oasis**, where we will dine in the style of a Batavian gentleman. Formal dress is not required but jeans and thongs would look distinctly out of place. Suitably attired, at 6 p.m. take a taxi to the **Hyatt Aryaduta** hotel on Jl. Prapatan in Menteng, for a sundown cocktail in the elegant **Ambassador Lounge** (to the right after the main door). Order a Planters Punch or other suitably Maughamesque beverage and listen to the genteel strains of chamber music filtering through the potted palms while clandestine lovers act nonchalant and businessmen finalize multi million dollar deals.

Jl. Surabaya, memoirs of old Batavia

Ask the doorman to fetch you a taxi (the buzzer is concealed in a flower bed), and take a short ride to Jl. Raden Saleh 47 where you will find a fine old Dutch mansion, now Oasis Restaurant. Be sure to order the house special, *Rijsttaffel* (rice table), a selection of Indonesian dishes served in succession by a column of *sarong*-clad waitresses while batak singers from north Sumatra serenade. Dinner at Oasis is the last vestige of the grand colonial lifestyle enjoyed by the Dutch in the heydays of the Dutch East India Company.

Dragons In Paradise

Buffet breakfast, a ramble through the Bogor Botanical Gardens, a country palace, noodles for lunch; a visit to a traditional gong factory; the legendary Komodo and Ragunan Zoo.

Today we do what Jakartans have been doing since colonial days to escape the city heat and clamour – head for the hills. The Dutch built their mountain resorts in the cool uplands south of Jakarta, surrounded by tea plantations, cold tumbling streams, and mist shrouded volcanoes.

Start with buffet breakfast around 8 a.m. at the **Sriwedari Garden** restaurant by the pool at the Hilton Hotel. At this time of day the gardens are beautiful, later in the day it's too hot to eat outside.

After breakfast go to the Bluebird Taxi stand on the right outside the main door of the hotel, and hire a taxi by the hour (around Rp10,000), or if you are with friends, a minibus for the day. (Bluebird at the Hilton is reliable, easy to find and reasonably priced but you may also hire a car through your hotel or ask around for the best rates.)

Drive out of Jakarta along the new toll road through flat rice fields to the foothills of **Bogor**, about 45 minutes away. Proceed to the **Botanical Gardens (Kebun Raya)** which, along with the presidential palace, form the heart of this pleasant city of villas, green spreading trees and afternoon thunderstorms.

Stop at the information booth to the right of the main entrance to the Gardens and pick up a leaflet and map. You can hire a guide if you wish but you can easily find your way around with the map. Spend a couple of hours walking in the gardens which were laid out under the direction of Stamford Raffles during his period as Governor General of Batavia and which contain a huge collection of flora from all over the world. There are pools filled with giant lotus leaves, orchid hothouses, weird twisting vines, a river rushing over black rocks, monkeys, hidden glades, grassy vales. During the week the park is pleasantly empty and you may happily lose yourself along the many winding paths through the trees. Finish up with a look at the memorial to Raffles' wife, Olivia Mariamme, then walk further down the path to emerge before the rear lawn of the **palace**, built as a country house by Dutch Governor General Baron Gustaf Willem van Imhoff. Glamorous house parties took place here during the colonial period, spotted deer still graze beneath spreading trees in the grounds.

The palace is currently used as an alternative state palace by President Suharto; in 1989 it hosted the first Jakarta Informal Meeting on Kampuchea.

Back near the main gate, if

Bogor Botanical Garden

you are so inspired, make your way through the **Zoological Museum**. Then drive a short way up Jl. Juanda, turn right down Jl. Empang and right again at the bottom of the hill into Jl. Pulo, which turns a corner and crosses the river to become Jl. Pancasan. At No. 17 stop to visit a very medieval-looking **gong foundry** where *gamelan* gongs are still produced by traditional methods. The dark workshop with an earthen floor is lit by the glow of fires and crucibles of molten copper and filled with the disembodied notes of the gongsmiths' rhythmic hammering. If you have a friend who can ship it home to you, you may order your own *gamelan*, or perhaps a single hand-beaten gong.

Take the reverse route back to the top of Jl Empang but instead of turning left into Jl. Juanda, go straight on along Jl. Otto Iskandardinata and turn right into the main shopping street of Bogor, Jl. Surya Kencana. Stop for lunch at **Tan Ek Tjoan Bakery and Restaurant**, on the right at No. 157 (also has a clean restroom.) Order noodles with chicken and soup (*bakmi ayam pangsit*), or other noodle dishes and a fresh avocado juice. Finish up with ice cream and buy a box of home made cookies for the return journey.

Follow the main road back to Jakarta and instruct the driver to come into the city via **Ragunan Zoo**. Spend the afternoon in this pleasantly unstructured garden with plenty of trees and an interesting population of creatures including Sumatran tigers, giant pythons and the relative of the dinosaurs – the Komodo dragon.

A trip up-country usually leaves you feeling fresh but tired out. Return to your hotel for a therapeutic Tropical Nap and then if you're still up to it, round off this full day with dinner and a spectacular view of Jakarta by night at the **Sky Garden Restaurant**, top floor of the Nusantara Building. Easy to find, next door to the President Hotel on Jl. Thamrin by the Hotel Indonesia roundabout.

Right, Welcom Monum

Zoo entrance

Pick & Choose

Because of Jakarta's heavy traffic, the only practical way to sightsee is in geographic blocks. Half a morning can be wasted in getting from A to B if the traffic decides to jam up. That said, the itineraries are also composed with a loose theme in mind, and are not listed in order of importance, so read through first and see which appeals. Some itineraries can be linked with an afternoon itinerary in the same general area; where applicable, this is mentioned at the end of the tour.

A.M. Itineraries

1. Fine Art

A relaxing meander through leafy South Jakarta, visiting art galleries; craft browsing; precious gems; rattan furniture making; a Korean lunch.

Kemang is a suburb of South Jakarta which has grown up among the banana trees. *Kampongs* (traditional villages) tucked away down red earth paths exist alongside large, modern houses. It is a pleasant mix of old and new where smart galleries, shops and restaurants rub shoulders with vendors' stalls and cottage industries. A strongly Muslim area, there is a *musholla* (small mosque) on almost every corner, veiled women and the white hat of the *Haji* are a frequent sight.

Instruct your taxi to take you to **Jl. Bangka I** in Kemang, via Warung Buncit. Jl. Bankga I is a

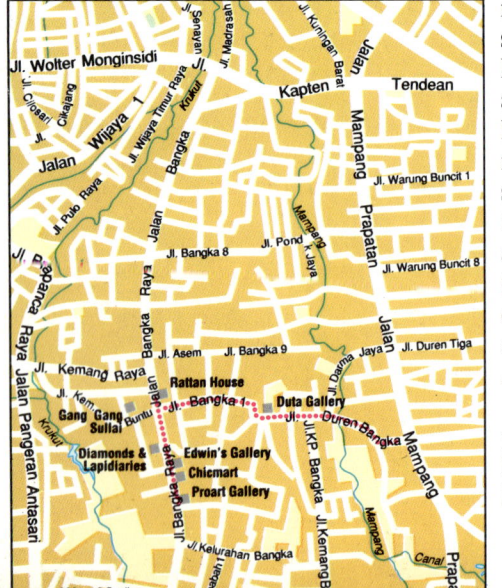

Edwin at his Gallery

long road which you can enter from either end, so enter the Buncit end. You turn off the main road, Jl. Warung Buncit Raya, into a smaller road, Jl. Duren Bangka which winds downhill to become Jl. Bangka I. First stop is at number 55a, **Duta Fine Arts Foundation**. Co-founded and managed by the French artist, Dhamelier, **Duta Gallery** is built in the style of a Mediterranean villa and stands in one of the prettiest gardens in Jakarta, with fountains, butterflies flitting in the sunshine and stone walls cascading with bougainvillaea. A series of cool whitewashed gallery rooms with terracotta floors house an extensive collection of paintings by Indonesian artists. The gallery also holds an exhibition, featuring a different artist, each month. High quality postcard reproductions can be bought just inside the front entrance.

The garden of Duta Gallery is linked by a gate to the **house of Kartini Basuki**, an Indonesian artist whose husband founded Duta Gallery with Dhamelier. If the gate is open you can catch a glimpse of another Mediterranean villa with a fine garden.

From Duta Gallery, proceed along Jl. Bangka I until it intersects with Jl. Kemang Raya. Turn left and continue to **Edwin's Gallery** at No. 21.

Chic Mart Handicraft

Edwins Gallery also houses a collection of Indonesian art but of more interest is the print room at the back where old lithographs and maps can be bought at very reasonable prices. For those who are interested but do not have a collector's budget, reproductions are available in the form of greeting cards.

Further along Jl. Kemang Raya, stop at **Chic Mart**, a rather incongruous pink building at No. 55. Inside is a refined range of high quality hand-made goods: cushions, plates painted with Balinese birds, porcelain, jewellery, wood, hand-painted sheets etc.

Art enthusiasts may wish to continue a few doors further down to **ProArt** at No. 67, another small art gallery.

When you've seen enough, drive back along Jl. Kemang Raya. For jewellery stop at **Diamonds and Lapidaries** at No. 30. Avoid the imported costume jewellery which is expensive. Better value are the real thing: rubies, emeralds, sapphires and the like, set as rings, necklaces etc. About 1 km (0.6 mile) further along is the Circle K store on the corner of Jl. Bangka Selatan. Opposite Circle K is **Gang Gang Sullai**, a Korean restaurant with a pleasant interior and excellent food. Just before you have lunch, cross over Jl. Bangka Raya for a look at **Rattan House**, No. 9A, where you can see craftsmen working on rattan furniture at the back. Back at Gang Gang Sullai, relax in air-conditioned comfort over tasty appetizers while the waiter cooks a delicious Korean barbecue for you at the table.

2. Menteng Morning

A walking tour around Menteng for batik, crafts, a modern glimpse of old Batavia, souvenir shirts, lunch al fresco.

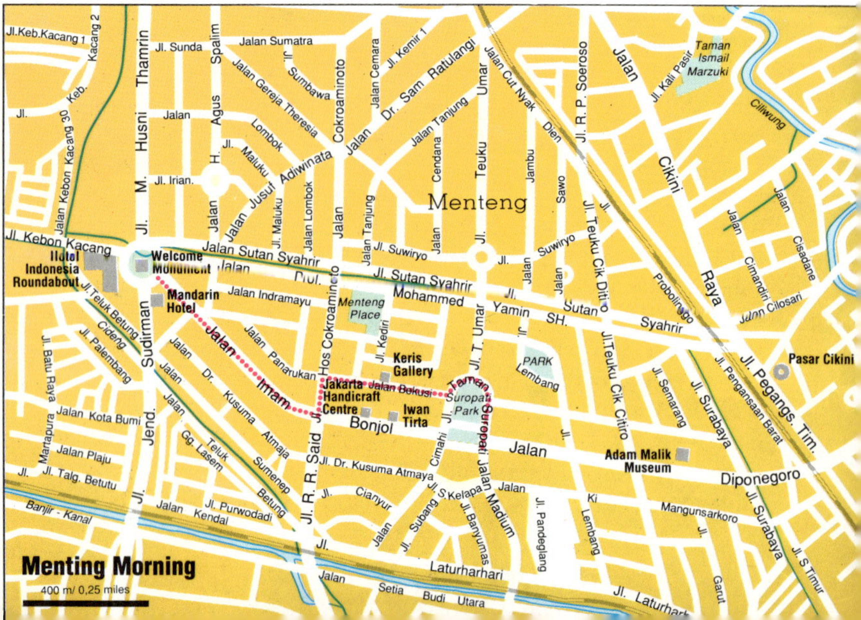

Menting Morning
400 m / 0.25 miles

At Iwan Tirta

Menteng is Jakarta's "old money" suburb, its tree shaded streets lined with solid Dutch villas with high-pitched roofs, leaded panes and shutters. Still an elite residential district, Menteng is where the President and many government officials have their homes.

From the Hotel Indonesia roundabout, walk one block down on the left of Jl. Imam Bonjol. Cross the first street on the left, Jl. H. Agus Salim, then walk down it a few metres to Jl. Pekalongan, a quiet, residential street on your right. At No. 12A, you will find the **Jakarta Handicraft Centre**, an air-conditioned showroom with a collection of handicrafts from throughout Indonesia. The quality of workmanship is strictly supervised and as the main focus of the business is export, wooden items are treated so they will endure in a different climate. If you are thirsty, a complimentary drink is offered in the garden at the rear.

Continue along Jl. Pekalongan and turn right into Jl. Panarukan. Stop at **Iwan Tirta's** shop at No. 25. If Jim Thompson was the King of Thai Silk, Iwan Tirta is the Prince of Batik. A lawyer turned fashion designer, his innovative approach to the traditional textile art produced a more modern and colourful fabric suited to international tastes. Now favoured by diplomats and society wives, Iwan Tirta's silk *batiks* command international prices, but are among the most beautiful Indonesia has to offer.

Walk along to the end of Jl. Panarukan where it meets a main road, Jl. H.O.S. Cokroaminoto. Turn left and walk past the Hero Supermarket (where you will find most sundry items if in need) and on until you are level with **Menteng Plaza**, a lime-green building on the opposite side of the main road. Cross over and take the escalator to **Hani and Roberts Village** on the first floor. Billed as a return to the nostalgia of old Batavia, "streets" in H&R Village have names like Oud Gondangdia and Prinsenpark. Shops sell trivia and souvenir T-shirts with slogans like "The Sun Didn't Shine Until God Created Indonesia".

Taman Senapati

From H&R Village, escalate down and out, turn left and walk on a few metres to **Apotik Jawa**. Poke your head in for a look at old apothecary jars in a quaint, dim, old world dispensary. A couple of doors along is **Keris Gallery**, a glass-fronted department store. The ground floor features expensive imported designer clothes and cosmetics. The second floor, however, has a very good selection of *batik* and other traditional fabrics, inexpensive ready-made *batik* clothes and a wide selection of interesting handicrafts. The third floor features women's clothing by leading Indonesian designers and is the only shop in Jakarta which has fitting rooms big enough for Westerners.

When you've exhausted the possibilities in Keris Gallery, walk on one short block past vendors cooking a curious selection of fried things, onto the corner of Jl. Basuki. Turn left and walk a few yards (metres) to the restaurant called **Tan Goei**. Take a seat outside for atmosphere, inside for air-conditioning.

Specialities of the house are chicken *sate* and the best fresh yoghurt drink in the capital. Unless you like your drink SWEET, order with sugar syrup on the side and mix to taste. Ambrosial. After lunch walk on up Jl. Basuki to emerge on **Taman Suropati**. The beautiful villa on the corner to your right is now the Residence of the U.S. Ambassador. A substantial liquor cache buried during the Japanese occupation is rumored to still reside in an unknown location in the garden. Walk round the half moon Taman past other Dutch mansions to reach the main road, Jl. Imam Bonjol. Turn right and walk back up to the Hotel Indonesia Roundabout.

3. Indonesia In Miniature

A visit to Indonesia's giant cultural theme park plus a memorable movie inside the Golden Snail.

Taman Mini Indonesia Indah, or **Beautiful Indonesia in Miniature Park**, is a cultural theme park located just south of Jakarta. For visitors who do not have the time to travel the length and breadth of the archipelago (few Indonesians even manage it), Taman Mini offers an insight into the country's extraordinary ethnic diversity and the fascinating blend of architectural styles, social customs and arts of the 27 different provinces.

A highlight of a visit to Taman Mini is the film *Indonesian Indah*, which is shown on a giant Imax screen, the largest in Asia. Indonesia is a spectacularly beautiful country more than blessed with natural wonders. The Imax experience is as close as you can get to the real thing without actually climbing volcanoes or fighting through jungles.

Head for Taman Mini after breakfast. The trip takes about 15 minutes along the new Jagowari toll road. On weekdays you may drive through Taman Mini but you get a better view and it's more fun to take the cable car. Buy a ticket at the cable car station on the right after you enter the main gates.

The cable car ride will give you an idea of the park's layout so that you can orient your way around on foot. You will pass over a lake containing a network of islands that forms the shape of the Indonesian archipelago and the centre of the park. Get off the cable car at station B and visit the **Bird Park** which should not be missed. Designed with inspiration, the park consists of a series of interconnecting geodesic domes forming a giant cage which you walk through, meeting the birds in something very close to their natural habitat.

From the Bird Park, make your way back through the rest of the park on foot. There is too much to see in half a day, and a full day of culture can become a surfeit, so take a sampling approach and meander. Back at the front entrance check the screening times of the Imax movie in **Keong Mas**, the building shaped like a large golden snail. While waiting for the show to begin, visit the **Museum Indonesia**, a large Balinese style building on the other side of the main park entrance which contains a well-presented display of handicrafts and artifacts.

A visit to Taman Mini can be extended to a full day.

Taman Mini

Marina Ancol

4. Bay Morning

Breakfast at the beach; browsing in a seaside art market; dolphins on show.

Unless it is Sunday, make an early start (7 a.m.) to beat the traffic through Chinatown where mid-morning traffic jams render the area a hellish blend of heat, blue exhaust fumes and blaring horns.

Take a taxi to Ancol and ask to be dropped at the **Horison Hotel**, a 20-minute ride if the roads are clear. The Horison is Jakarta's only waterfront hotel, rather odd decor but in the coffee shop you can have breakfast and watch skiffs with big triangular sails pass by on the Jakarta Bay. Be sure to order the Horison's warm almond croissants which cannot be beat this side of Paris. Follow breakfast with a walk on the beach.

Leave the hotel by the front entrance and turn left. Follow the road round until you reach the large swimming pool complex. Across the road on your right is **Pasar Seni**, the arts and crafts market, which opens around 10 o'clock. The market consist of a number of shops, nicely laid out with pathways among the palm trees. In many of the shops, artisans from all over Indonesia can be seen at work, making *batik*, silverware and puppets, painting, carving wood and making shell ornaments. If you feel so inclined you can sit for your portrait in pastels or even commission a work in oils.

When you have seen enough, proceed to the **Oceanarium**, next door to the swimming pool complex. Dolphin shows occur at regular intervals; sit on tiered benches and order a lemonade

Ancol Oceanarium

ice block to cool off while the dolphins play ball, demonstrate their ability to count and answer questions.

Return to Pasar Seni for lunch and take your pick of the restaurants serving good and inexpensive Indonesian food. Try *nasi campur*, a typical Indonesian meal-on-one-plate, consisting of white rice, fried chicken, a skewer or two of *sate*, pickles, *sambal*, and a large shrimp cracker. Wash it down with a cold Bintang beer.

Those with children, or who still feel like children, may wish to stay on at Ancol through the afternoon, at the swimming pool complex with giant slides, artificial rapids etc, or at **Dunia Fantasy**, S.E. Asia's largest fun park. Dunia Fantasy is clean, pleasantly laid out and has a particularly electrifying (and well maintained) double corkscrew rollercoaster. A ride should be mandatory for anyone who thinks the world had become too tame a place. Children will also enjoy dinner in **Apung Restaurant**, a model *pinisi* schooner, "anchored" at the Ancol Marina, still in the complex but a little further round the bay.

5. Antique Hunt

Treasure hunting in Ciputat village; lunch beside a lake.

This is a trip for the dedicated antique and artifact buyer and for browsers who like poking around in dusty shops full of curiosities. It's a hot and grubby exercise so dress in loose clothes and wear comfortable shoes. A water bottle and a pack or two of cologne wipes will extend your endurance considerably. Relaxation comes at the end of the line with an *al fresco* lunch.

Leave town around 9 a.m. and direct your car or taxi to **Jl. Ciputat Raya**. The drive takes about 20 minutes if there are no traffic

Ciputat antique shop

jams. You will pass through the southern suburbs of Jakarta to reach the semi rural area of Ciputat. You will pass through the gateway to West Java (Java Barat); another landmark is the Hero supermarket which you will pass on your left shortly before Situ Gintung village. The main road as it passes through Situ Gintung is lined on both sides with antique shops selling furniture, ceramics, textiles, ethnic jewellery, artifacts and all manner of cabbages and kings.

Start your hunt when the first antique shops start to appear. Walk and drive along for a couple kilometres, stopping at the various clusters of shops where you will see workmen rubbing down old Javanese wedding chests, restoring Dutch four-poster beds and re-weaving rattan chair backs. You may want to zig-zag across the road and have a late lunch, or work your way up the left side and do the right side on the way back after lunch.

The shops come to an end at the top of a rise where you will see a big sign on the left saying KOLAM RENANG. Walk through the **Situ Gintung Kuring** restaurant door and you will emerge on a grassy slope which drops down to a lake. Order your meal at the top of the hill, it will be delivered to the table of your choice. Specialities of the house are excellent baked fish (*ikan bakar*), fried chicken (*ayam goreng*), vegetable in tamarind soup (*sayur asem*) and young coconut juice served in the nut (*es kelapa muda*). The best method is to order a selection of dishes (fish by the kilo), spread them out on the table and share. Fingerbowls and napkins are provided; creating piles of fish and chicken bones in the middle of the table is accepted etiquette.

After lunch work your way down the other side of the road, or if you have had enough, head back to Jakarta. To avoid traffic jams you should not leave Ciputat later than 3.30 p.m.

6. Textile Tour

Breakfast and a walk by the lake; a visit to a batik factory; two historical houses; the textile museum, more batik; fish head curry and a historic graveyard.

Start with an 8 a.m. buffet breakfast at the **Peacock Cafe** in the Hilton Hotel. Save a bread roll and after breakfast walk through the gardens and around the ornamental lake where your offering

Batik Hajadi, intricate handmade fabric

will attract herons, swans and ducks grooming themselves in the morning sunshine among frangipani trees and water lilies.

Return to the lobby and take a taxi to Jl. Kebayoran Lama via Jl. Palmerah Barat. After you turn into Jl. Kabayoran Lama, you must pay attention to the right hand side of the road or you will miss the small turn-off into Jl. Mesjid Palmerah VII, which occurs after about 1 km (0.6 miles). This street is also marked on some maps as Jl. Berdikari Mesjid Al Dawah. The turn is marked by a clear sign saying "Batik Berdikari".

Batik Berdikari is at No. 7B on the right. Tours of the factory can be arranged at the desk, no charge. The fine art of wax-resist dyeing has been refined to its highest form in Indonesia, particularly in Java. The wax is heated over a burner and poured into bamboo and copper quills called *chanting*, used to trace the beautiful birds, flowers and geometrics that characterize Batik Tulis, hand painted batik. *Batik Cap* is made by printing the fabric with an intricate copper stamp. The process may involve several waxings and dyeings before the cloth is finally washed and hung in the sun to dry.

When you leave Batik Berdikari, drive up to the end of the street and turn round in front of the mosque. On the way there and back you will pass a number of plant nurseries selling bamboos, bougainvillaea, palms, pots and other gardening materials. Stop and wander through if the mood takes you.

Back at the main road, turn left and drive back along Jl. Kebayoran Lama to Jl. Palmerah Barat. On the corner where Jl. Palmerah Barat becomes Jl. Palmerah, keep a look out for the police station, housed in an old two-storey building set back off the road. History buffs should stop for a look at **Gedung Tinggi** (High House), formerly the country house of one Andries Hartsinck, a rich Batavian who owned several estates.

From Gedung Tinggi, proceed along Jl. Palmerah and turn left at

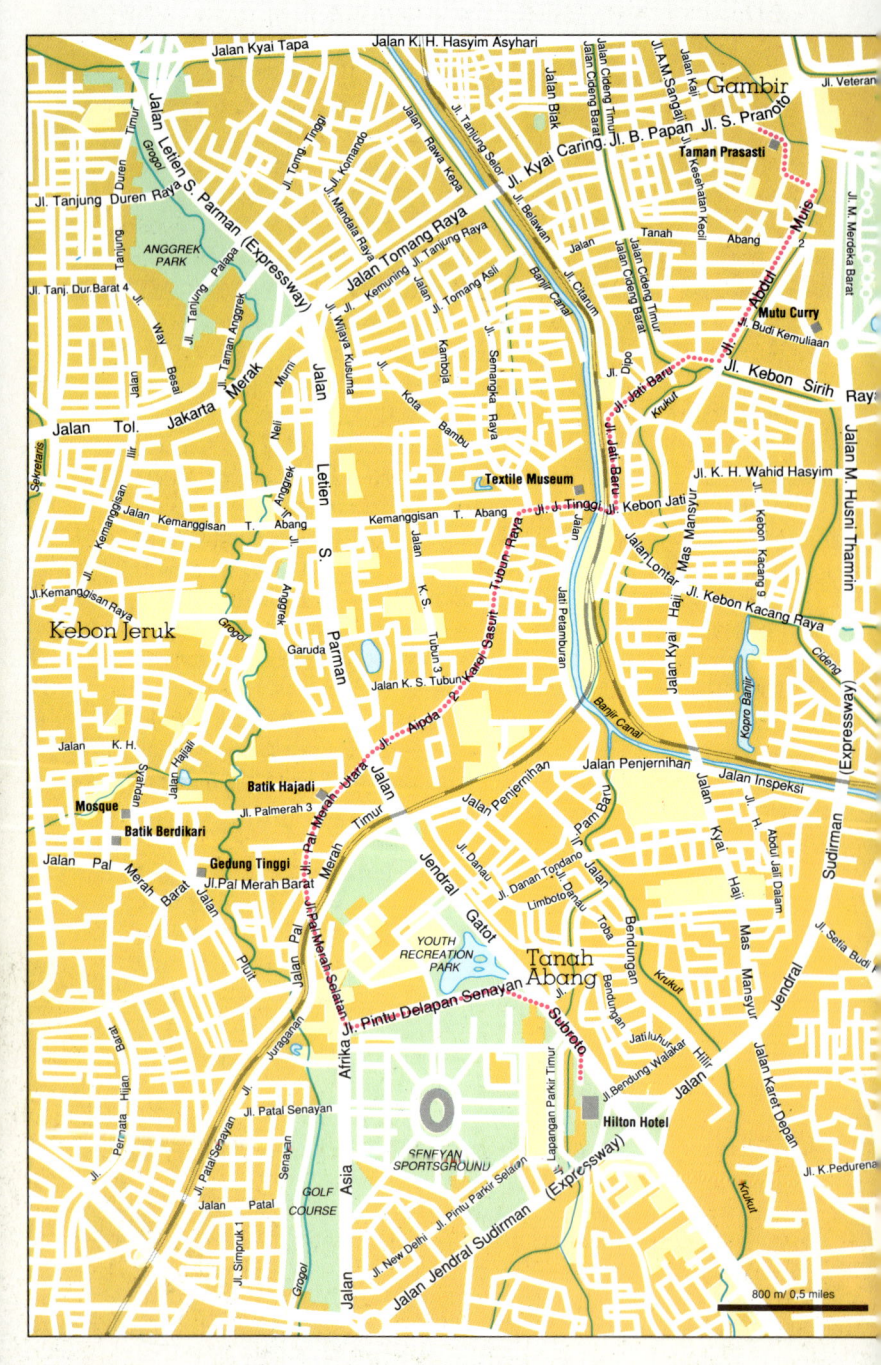

the intersection with Jl. Palmerah Utara. Stop at **Batik Hajadi**, on the left at No. 46, where you will find a wide range of *batik*, *ikat* (traditional woven cottons) and printed cotton upholstery fabrics. The prices are so reasonable it is worth buying yardage to take home for curtain making, cushions etc. Attractive ready-made cushion covers and quilts are for sale on the first floor, tablecloths and mats, clothes and knick-knacks on the ground floor.

From Batik Hajadi follow Jl. Palmerah Utara until it crosses under the toll road and becomes Jl. A.K. Satsuit Tuban. At No. 4, on a corner just before the bridge, stop at the **Textile Museum**, housed in the 19th century house of a French resident of Batavia. A very fine collection of textiles from all over Indonesia shows the sophistication of the fabric arts which have been developed in different regional styles over hundreds of years. Indonesia's textile heritage is one of the richest in the world.

From the Textile Museum continue over the bridge and follow the road through the crowded and bustling **Tanah Abang** market. Head for Jl. Tanah Abang Timur and ask the driver to let you out at **Tanamur**, Jakarta's most (in)famous nightspot. Next door to Tanamur is **Mutu Curry**, a light and airy Indian restaurant. Speciality of the house is fish head curry served on banana leaf plates.

Take a little time after lunch to visit **Taman Prasasti Cemetery**, the graveyard of early Batavian residents, a short distance away on Jl. Tanah Abang I (turn left off Jl. Abdul Muis). Now a quiet memorial park Taman Prasasti is the resting place of many historical figures including Olivia Miriamme Raffles, wife of the founder of Singapore and Governor General of Batavia during the colony's brief British period, Thomas Stamford Raffles.

Tanah Abang Market

P.M. Itineraries

1. Easy Afternoon

A market for birds, fruit, fish and flowers; fruit refresher; pampering massage.

Take a taxi to Jl. Kyai Maja in Kebayoran and get out at the intersection with Jl. Barito, which is at the end of the **bird market**. Walk up the right side of Jl. Barito where you will see cages containing a variety of brightly-coloured birds, screeching cockatoos, tethered birds of prey, boxes of live crickets and maggots, and other gourmet fare fancied by our feathered friends.

The bird stalls give way to fruit stalls towards the top end of the street. Conical piles of brilliant tropical fruit will make your mouth water – rambutan, *salak*, *jeruk bali*, melons, oranges, bananas, coconuts. You may ask to sample the wares before you buy, or just chat to the vendors. Markets are for socializing too.

Cross Jl. Barito when you see fish tanks on the other side. Here you can buy all kinds of fish and some interesting tank ornaments such as Chinese pagodas and flatulent mermaids. Follow the tanks around the corner into Jl. Mendawai. At the corner of Jl. Mendawai and Jl. Lamandau you will find a small **flower market** overflowing with purple orchid sprays, crimson roses, striped tiger orchids, delicate miniature yellow orchids, lilies, chrysanthemums and others. Purchase a few stems of *sedap malam* (night scented tuberose) at around Rp500 each.

Walk back to Jl. Barito, cross over the intersection and walk up Jl. Melawai Raya to Blok M. Cross over Jl. Panglima Polim to reach **Juice 88** at 116E Jl. Melawai Raya. Refresh yourself with

Flowers at the Market

fruit whips blended as you wait or *es campur*, a delicious concoction of crushed ice, coconut, avocado and other fresh fruit, topped off with condensed milk.

From **Blok** M, take a taxi to Jl. Cisanggiri in Pasar Santa, about 10 minutes away. At the end of Jl. Cisanggiri, turn right and immediately opposite at No. 10 is **Bon Vita** Health Massage.

For Rp6500 per hour (90 minutes is a good workout) you will experience one of the best revival treatments in Jakarta. Bon Vita is not a fancy massage parlour but it is clean, straight, gives great massage and caters for both men and women. Take a couple of *sedap malam* blossoms in with you and place them on the pillow. Their heady scent will add to the sensual pleasure. You will be offered a shower or a hot towel at the end of the session – take the rub down.

A trip to Bon Vita is recommended after any hard day of sightseeing. Stretch your legs a bit afterwards with a short walk through **Pasar Santa**, a small and friendly neighbourhood market selling fruit, and sundries, back to the main road, Jl. Wolter Monginsidi.

2. Blok M

A tour of Blok M shopping precinct; antiques, arts and crafts; Indonesian culinary extravaganza.

This shopping and browsing tour is equally suitable in the morning, afternoon or even early evening.

Take a taxi to the large department store called **Pasaraya** in Blok M. Get out just before the booth where cars must pay to get in. Turn your back on Pasaraya and cross Jl. Sultan Hasanuddin, to your left to reach Bank Rakyat Indonesia. From the bank walk in the opposite direction to the traffic flow and take the first street on your right, **Jl. Pelatehan I**. Along this short street you will find a number of shops and galleries on either side, selling handicrafts,

Blok M

paintings, antiques, *batik*, furniture. **Hadiprana Galleries** at No. 38 has silk *batik*, jewellery and modern paintings. **Bangka Tin**, a pewter-like metal from the Bankga Islands, can be found at No.43.

Walk up one side and back along the other and then recross Jl. Sultan Hasannuddin to Pasaraya. Walk round to the right of Pasaraya and turn left in the narrow street behind it, Jl. Melawai III. Opposite Pasaraya at No. 4 you will find **Majapahit Art & Curio**, three floors of Indonesian antiques, artifacts and curios.

When you come out of Majapahit, turn left and left again past vendors selling fruit, suitcases and fake designer watches. You will pass two photographic stores and then two gold stores where you may buy reasonably priced earrings, rings, chains etc. The pieces will be weighed and a certificate of weight and carat issued with your purchase. N.B. Anything below 18 carat is not considered to have resale value.

Continue on round the corner into Jl. Melawai VIII and straight on to the next corner. Along the way you will pass narrow entrances into the **pasar** (traditional market), a warren of alleys where you can buy cheap costume jewellery, sewing fabrics and haberdashery, stationery, clothes, glasses, china, pillows and all manner of inexpensive sundry items. If you go in and get lost, head for the daylight and you will emerge either on the street you came in on, or the next one round the block.

Head on round the block back to **Pasaraya** (look skyward and you'll see the sign). Pasaraya is a treasure trove of handicrafts, especially on the third floor, excellent for souvenirs, gift buying or just browsing.

When you've had your fill of shopping, go down to the basement where you will find a supermarket and **restaurant complex** with stalls offering various speciality dishes from around the archipelago. You simply walk around and see what takes your fancy, give your order and take a seat. This is the famous Indonesian street food, produced under more hygienic conditions but tasting just as good and excellent value for money. Before you leave the basement, look in at the traditional medicine counter, just opposite the supermarket check-outs, where you can buy the famous Indonesian *jamu* herbal remedies, tonics, aphrodisiacs and cosmetics.

3. To Market To Market

One man's museum; exotic sights and smells in a traditional market; a colourful visit to Jakarta's major bird market.

At around 1 p.m. start from the Hotel Indonesia roundabout and head straight down Jl. Imam Bonjol to Jl. Diponegoro and stop in at No. 29, the home of Former Vice President and Foreign Minister **Adam Malik**. Fascinated with history and culture, the late Adam Malik assembled a very fine collection of rare porcelain now housed in the Fine Arts Museum. His home has also been turned into a museum displaying an eclectic collection of ceramics, wooden artifacts, antiques, paintings, icons, memorabilia. The museum is opened daily from 9 a.m. until 2 p.m., admission fee is Rp1,000 and photos may not be taken.

Continue on down Jl. Diponegoro to the next major intersection and turn left into Jl. Pegangsaan Timur. Stop at **Pasar Cikini** on the right side of the road. Pasar Cikini is a traditional Indonesian market where housewives come and buy everything from fruit, spices, beans, meat and fish to clothes, children's toys, woven baskets, terracotta pots and gold jewellery. The pasar is a bustling, cramped, seemingly chaotic place that recaptures the feeling of Jakarta as one of the great trading ports of the far east, mysterious, exotic, full of savoury (and not so savoury) smells and curious sights. A good place to find odd, inexpensive souvenirs, sample weird snacks and in modern guidebook jargon, a great photo opportunity.

From Pasar Cikini return along Jl. Pegangsaan Timur to the intersection with Jl. Diponegoro and turn left. When Jl. Diponegoro

Favourite feathered friend

Befriend a bird?

intersects with Jl. Salemba Raya, turn right and at the next major intersection, left into Jl. Pramuka.

Turn left into Jl. Pramuka Dalam to reach **Pasar Burung**, the bird market. Rows of stalls display cages containing the colourful, exotic birds of the tropics. The Perkutut or Java Turtledove is the most highly prized of birds, not for its feathers which are a rather unprepossessing dun colour, but for its legendary voice.

You will also see baby rabbits, guinea pigs, squirrels and monkeys, and more unusual creatures such as weasels, jungle cats, owls and eagles. Bargaining is the order of the day and the price does not include a cage. Birds purchased are handed over in a small, rustling brown paper bag.

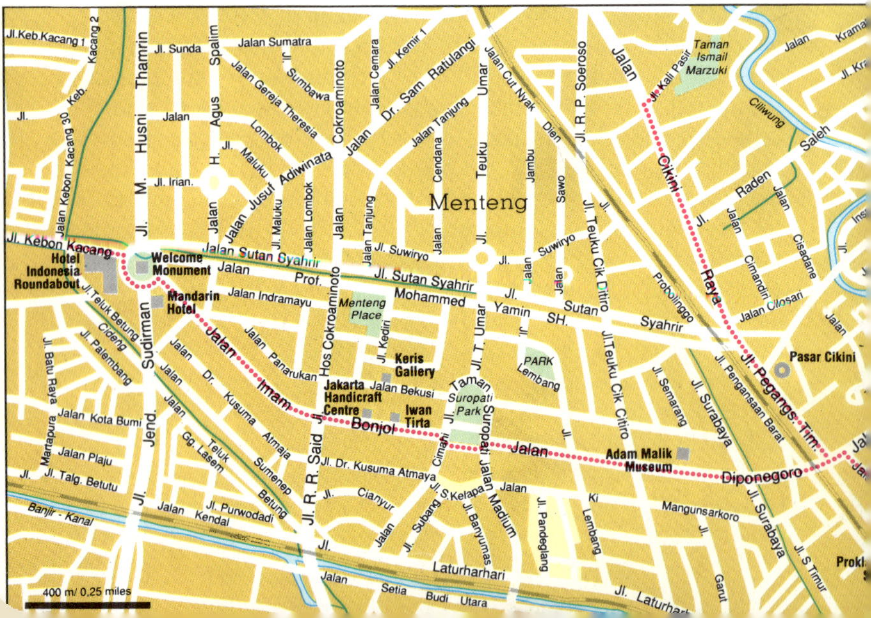

Return to the city via Jl. Matraman (straight on the intersection of Jl. Pramuka and Jl. Salemba Raya). Jl. Matraman soon becomes Jl. Proklamasi. Stop at **Taman Proklamasi** (Proclamation Park) on the left side of the road, to see a monument to the Fathers of Indonesian Independence, President Sukarno and Vice President Mohammad Hatta. In a house nearby on Jl. Pegangsaan, they declared Indonesian Independence on 17 August, 1945. Proklamasi, celebrated on that day yearly, is Indonesia's biggest national holiday.

Continue along Jl. Proklamasi to Jl. Diponegoro, turn left and follow the road back to your starting point at the Hotel Indonesia Roundabout.

4. Antiques And Tea

A leisurely afternoon of treasure hunting followed by an elegant afternoon tea and a walk in the park.

Take a taxi to **Jl. Kebun Sirih Timur Dalam**, a narrow street in central Jakarta that connects Jl. Wahid Hasyim with Jl. Kebon Sirih. The street is another of Jakarta's well-known antique alleys, also a one way thoroughfare and a popular short cut, usually jammed with traffic. Get out at the beginning of the street and criss-cross your way down, visiting the many antique and art shops for ceramics, textiles, wayang puppets, old gold jewellery and hair ornaments, wooden artifacts and carvings, stone statues and all manner of other fascinating things.

At the bottom of the street catch a taxi to the Borobudur Intercontinental Hotel on Jl. Lapangan Banteng Selatan. In the **Pendopo Lounge**, straight ahead as you come up the escalator, order high tea and a trolley of sandwiches and wicked cakes. If possible find a window seat overlooking the large landscaped garden and contemplate the bygone days of the spice empire as a chamber music ensemble provides appropriate musical accompaniment to the genteel mood.

After tea stroll along the **shopping arcade** (on two floors) where there are a number of good shops specializing in ethnic and modern jewellery, *batik*, antiques, paintings, gemstones, oriental rugs and more.

Outside the Hotel Borobudur, cross over into **Lapangan Banteng** (deer field), a green square laid out by Governor General Daendels whose early 19th-century palace now houses the **Ministry of Finance**. In front of the palace is a statue of a muscle-bound man breaking out of chains. This is Sukarno's monument to the liberation of Irian Jaya (New Guinea) from Dutch rule. Next door to the Department of Finance is the Supreme Court (**Mahkamah Agung**) which dates from 1848. Walk on round the park to the **Catholic Cathedral**, built at the beginning of this century, then complete the circle by returning to Hotel Borobudur.

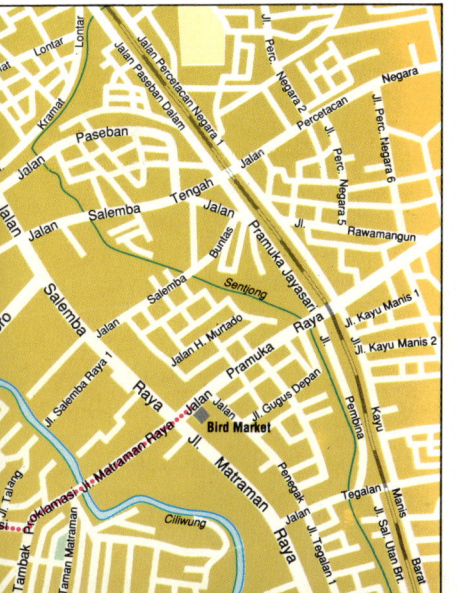

Nightlife

Jakarta nightlife is as varied as the city's inhabitants. The evening is a pleasant time to be abroad and Jakartans of all strata love to go out, if only to stroll about or sit and watch the world go by.

Restaurant kitchens tend to close early so plan to start dinner before 9 p.m. Clubs and bars stay open late and supper in the early hours of the morning is the traditional way to wind up a night on the town.

Sin is readily available for those who want it and avoidable for those who don't. Western men invariably attract "nice" Indonesian girls who wouldn't normally be in this bar except that...wallets and hearts can get lost. There is no reason why Western women shouldn't go out on the town but they will have to deal with the widely accepted notion that they have a lower moral standard than their Asian counterparts. A polite refusal of unwanted attentions is usually sufficient to deter most Indonesian would-be-Romeos, who were raised in a courteous culture, and pointed in the right direction, will usually revert to type.

1. Cultural Pursuits

For a night on the town sampling Jakarta's cultural offerings, start out in the early evening with *gamelan* music in the lobby of the **Hilton Hotel**. After dinner visit **Bharata Theatre** at Jl. Pasar Senen 15 for traditional Javanese *wayang orang* and *ketoprak* theatre performances (8 p.m. nightly except Saturday). Traditional shadow puppet performances, *wayang kulit*, can be seen at the **National Museum** on the second and fourth Saturdays of the month (all night). **Taman Ismail Marzuki,** located on Jl. Cikini Raya 73 in Menteng, is the culture and performing arts centre of Jakarta where you can see dance, theatre, music, painting exhibitions, poetry readings etc. The complex includes a number of halls, theatres, cinemas and a planetarium. A monthly calendar of events is available at the centre and selected programs are listed daily in the *Jakarta Post* newspaper.

For a touch of nostalgia, take in a show (usually dance or music) at **Gedung Kesenian** on the corner of Jl. Pos and Jl. Kesenian. Recently restored to its original glory, the former Dutch colonial **Schouwberg playhouse** is worth a visit for the place as much as the

JI. Sabang

performance. Alternatively, situated inside the Jaya Ancol Dreamland complex, the Art Market **Pasar Seni** also features many traditional performing arts as well as shops selling a wide range of handicrafts and paintings. With open air restaurants, paved boulevards and a breeze from the sea, a very pleasant place to while away an evening. Classic supper clubs include the **Blue Ocean** on Jl. Hayam Wuruk, a Chinese fantasy with an elaborate floorshow, and the more sedate **Nirwana Supper Club** in the Hotel Indonesia.

2. More Trivial Pursuits

An excellent vantage point from which to watch the sun set over Jakarta is the **Kon Tiki Bar** on the 16th floor of Wisma Metropolitan II, Jl. Jend. Sudirman. Unwind with a tropical cocktail and watch the sky turn vermillion while long lines of traffic crawl home along Jakarta's main artery, way below. Other pleasant places for pre-dinner drinks are the **Kudus Bar** of the Hilton Hotel, the **Pendopo Bar** of the Borobudur Intercontinental and the **Ambassador Lounge** of the Hyatt Aryaduta.

The **Pizzaria** by the lake in the Jakarta Hilton is one of the few places where you can dine out of doors in the evening. A live band performs every night with Reggae night on Tuesday. Live music and pub meals also available at **The Tavern** (Hyatt Aryaduta Hotel), a very popular venue. Country & Western music plus first grade margaritas and south-of-the-border cuisine at **Amigos** (Kemang Club Villas complex) and **Green Pub** (Djakarta Theatre building). Disco/ bar/ restaurants include **Topaz** (Jl. Rasuna Said), **Temptation** (Jl. Kemang Raya), **Galactica** (Jl. Asia Africa) and **Parrots** (Jl. Wahid Hasyim).

Bars which come into their own later at night are the **Captain's Bar** (Mandarin Oriental Hotel) which features live bands and often an impromptu jam session by local musos, and the **Melati Lounge**

(Sari Pan Pacific Hotel) which specializes in imported jazz and some great local jazz by aging *angklung* musicians. For Western-style entertainment, the **Chicago Entertainment Club** and **Top Gun** in Blok M are popular. Oil workers like the **King's Head** and **Dirgantara**, serious watering holes in Kebayoran.

Pete's Tavern (Wisma Argo Menunggal on Jl. Gatot Subroto) and **Jaya Pub** (Jl. M.H. Thamrin) are owned and run by Indonesia's most famous film star couple, Frans Tambuan and Rima Melati. Both offer live music and pub food. The Jaya Pub is always crowded and raging, Pete's is bigger and accommodates a crowd with more comfort.

No night on the town in Jakarta is complete without a visit to **Tanamur** (Jl. Tanah Abang Timur), the city's legendary first disco; the dance floor reputed to be the most densely populated spot in the most densely populated archipelago. After 10.30 p.m. it's standing room only and after 11.30 p.m. standing-on-one-foot room only. Loud, smoky, raging and no place to take your grandmother. **The Oriental** (Hilton Hotel) and **The Music Room** (Borobudur Intercontinental) are also very popular discos, always full to capacity on weekends and Ladies Night. **The Pitstop** (Sari Pan Pacific) is a smaller disco with a live band where you can normally get a table or a seat at the bar (no jeans). For a taste of ancient Egypt, **Ebony** (jl. Rasuna Said) has a live band and waitresses in Nubian dress. **Stardust** (Kota) is a huge converted cinema favoured by Chinese teens. Most discos have a cover charge which includes the first drink.

Many discos and bars close at around 1 a.m. After that, dedicated party goers continue to Blok M where within a narrow radius are **Tambora**, **K Bar**, **The Club**, and **Sundowners**. In these low-brow establishments oil workers and bar girls mix like cocktail ingredients, cruisers of all persuasions pursue their particular tastes.

When the night's energy has passed its peak, recuperation is had in the **Peacock Coffee Shop** (Hilton), **Ramayana Terrace** (Hotel Indonesia) and the **Bogor Brasserie** (Borobudur Intercontinental). Recommended late-night pick-me-ups include *bubur ayam* (chicken porridge), *mie kangkung* (noodles, quail eggs and swamp greens) and *sop buntut* (oxtail soup). Cheaper, traditional early morning food is found in the all-night warungs on **Jl. Kendal**. For the adventurous, a most savoury dish is a comforting soup made from sheep parts, including eye and other balls.

Day Trips

Anyone spending more than a couple of days in Jakarta should try to get out of the city for a day or overnight trip. Most of Jakarta's major sites can be seen in a couple of days and there are some beautiful places within easy striking distance of the capital which will provide a relaxing break from the bustling heat of the city.

1. Hill Safari

Full Day

From colonial times until the present, Jakartans have made weekend getaways into the cool green hills south of the city, about two hours away by car. The road through the Puncak Pass snakes its way steeply up, through hills planted with stubby tea bushes, villages lined with guesthouses, verandahs tumbling with bougainvillaea and roadside stalls piled with fresh vegetables grown robust in the rich volcanic earth and cool climate.

Spend the morning in the **Safari Park**, well signposted from the main road (crowded on weekends), to see exotic Indonesian and imported wildlife in an extensive, naturally landscaped park renowned for its successful breeding program.

After lunch in the park, return to the main Puncak road and continue up the hill. Stop and walk a little wherever the fancy takes you; enjoy the invigorating mountain air and the cool weather flowers: jasmine, marigolds and even rambling roses. Just over the summit

Safari Park

is the **Puncak Pass Hotel**, a compulsory stop for afternoon tea on the way back. Follow the winding road down through green valleys and mountain villages to Cipanas. On the right side of the road is **Istana Cipanas**, a beautiful Victorian holiday house belonging to the President, surrounded by pretty gardens. Overnight travellers may stay at one of the guesthouses signposted in Cipanas and hike up nearby volcano Gunung Gede (start at dawn).

Day trippers should visit the **Botanical Gardens** at **Cibodas** (turn-off signposted on the main road) before turning around for Jakarta. On the homeward journey call in at the **Puncak Pass Hotel**. In the dry season take a seat outside and look down over rural Java; in the rainy season sit inside and watch Scottish mists swirl through the purple hills. To complete the experience order hot cocoa, banana pancakes with maple syrup and *poffertjes* – Dutch dough balls fried and dusted with powdered sugar, none of which are listed on the menu but all of which are legendary in taste.

Leave before it gets dark and travel back down through the dusk when the village lamps are being lit and men in sarongs lead ponies back from the fields. Stop at roadside stalls on the way down to buy melons, bananas, carrots, radishes and a traditional gift for friends who stayed behind in Jakarta.

2. Colonial Island Picnic

Full Day

Several islands in the Jakarta Bay were used by the Dutch in colonial times, both as resorts and naval depots. **Pulau Bidadari**, once the site of a fort and a leper's hospital, has been turned into a resort island with bungalows and a restaurant. **Ferries** leave for Pulau Bidadari from the Ancol Marina every day at 10 a.m. and 9 a.m. on weekends (Fare Rp10,000). There is no need to book but you should arrive at the Bidadari Terminal half an hour before the boat departs. Allow at least half an hour to get to Ancol from central Jakarta.

From Pulau Bidadari you can take a boat trip around the nearby islands which also have links with the colonial past. **Pulau Onrust** is the site of a 17th-century shipyard where Dutch East India traders once docked for repairs after the long haul from Europe and where the first Governor General of Batavia, Jan Pieterzoon Coen, marshalled his fighting ships. A small fort, hospital, church and artillery store completed the VOC shipyard. Neighbouring **Pulau Kelor, Pulau Kahyangan, and Pulau Damar** also have historical links with the VOC maritime industry. One of the earliest residents of Jakarta to appreciate the potential of the islands as a private paradise was Governor General Camphuis, who in 1685 built a fine and much-talked-of Japanese-style villa on Pulau Damar amid gardens stocked with rare animals and plants.

Wan De Yuan Temple

3. Old Banten

In the 16th century the Sultanate of Banten was a powerful trading empire on the northwest coast of Java. The Banten port was a centre of the pepper trade and flourished until the neighbouring port of Sunda Kelapa, which was conquered by the Sultan of Banten with the help of the East Javanese Sultan of Demak, rose to take its place.

Banten was a cosmopolitan settlement peopled by Chinese, Arab and Indian traders as well as the local West Javanese. In 1527 the town was conquered by an Islamic leader, Hasanuddin, and in 1559 the **Agung Mosque** (Mesjid Agung) was built. The mosque, which has been restored, contains a small museum. The **Wan De Yuan Temple** not far from the mosque attracts pilgrims from near and far each year for a major Chinese festival.

Other relics of old Banten include a watchtower, all that remains of **Fort Speelwijk**, built by the Dutch in 1682, still with a commanding view. After years of raids and counter-raids between Banten and Batavia, the Dutch eventually conquered Banten and installed a puppet ruler. The arched walls of the **Surosowan Palace**, family residence of the last Sultan of Banten, are still standing.

It takes about two hours to reach Banten by car from Jakarta. A return trip including a picnic lunch makes a pleasant one-day excursion, or you may continue on to Carita Beach and Krakatau for an overnight stay. Coach trips to Banten are also available. Ask at your hotel or any travel agent.

4. The Thousand Islands

Overnight

One of Jakarta's saving graces, **Pulau Seribu** (the Thousand Islands) is a collection of coral atolls in the Java Sea north of Tanjung Priok harbour.

The contrast between this idyllic island getaway and the bustling, overheated atmosphere of the city have made Pulau Seribu a popular weekend resort, one that has been in use since colonial times.

It takes three hours by ferry, one hour by speedboat, or 20 minutes by plane to reach the islands. Several of the islands have been developed as tourist resorts but most have taken pains to retain the simplicity that makes the islands so attractive. During the week you will have most of the islands to yourself and many of the resorts offer reduced weekday rates.

Nearly all of the islands are edged with coral reefs, and snorkelling and scuba diving gear can be hired on the island. Coral novices beware of stings, abrasions, cuts and sunburn. It is advisable to cover arms and legs while swimming or snorkelling. The marine life in Pulau Seribu includes turtles, moray and garden eels, rays, pelagic and reef fish, nudibranch, anemones, giant clams, sea fans, soft and hard corals. Dolphins and flying fish can often be seen during the boat trip from Jakarta.

Pulau Putri and **Pulau Pelangi** have air-conditioned cottages, tennis courts and on Pelangi, a popular restaurant built on the water.

Ferries depart daily around 7 a.m. from the Ancol marina for the islands. The trip takes around 2½ hours and the return ferry leaves the islands around 2.30 in the afternoon the following day. Faster and slightly more expensive trips can be made by speedboat and hydrofoil which takes about an hour. Enquire at **Putri Pulau Seribu Paradise** booking office in Djakarta Theatre building or at your hotel. **Flights** to Pulau Seribu can be chartered at **Kemayoran airport**, or enquire through the resort booking offices.

Take sunscreen, insect repellent, shoes for walking on the reef, food if you don't want to take every meal in a restaurant. Look for fruit bats, big and small lizards, birds, butterflies, turtles, crabs, pearly island dawns, sunsets to weep over and occasionally, massive shooting stars.

Krakatau, view from Java Coast

5. Carita Beach And Krakatau

Full Day or Overnight

Carita Beach, a wide sweep of sand lined with coconut groves, overlooks the Sunda Straits towards Sumatra. It is popular for swimming and sunbathing on weekends but is pleasantly empty during the week. On a clear day you can see what remains of **Krakatau**, the legendary volcano that in 1883 rocked the world with a stupendous explosion and blew itself to smithereens.

It takes around 2½ hours to reach Carita from Jakarta. With a pre-dawn start you can make it a day trip but most people stay overnight in one of the many bungalow hotels. The most famous is **Krakatau Beach Hotel** which should be visited even if you opt to stay somewhere else. There are display boards explaining the eruption and you can arrange a boat trip to view **Anak Krakatau**, Son of Krakatau, the active core of the new volcano that was born out of the explosion. A smoking mound of red-black earth that rises out of the sea, Anak Krakatau rumbles and spits from time to time and even in its quieter moments has an eerie, cataclysmic presence.

On the way to Carita you will pass through **Anyer**, a smaller resort with an **historical lighthouse**. If you have strong leg muscles and a head for heights, stop and climb the 200-odd spiral steps to the top for a magnificent view of the Sunda Straits, the coconut groves along the coast and the mountainous hinterland.

Pelabuhan Ratu, mystical cave

From Carita you can take a one-day speed-boat trip or longer overnight trip to **Ujung Kulong**, the spectacular, unspoilt nature reserve on the southernmost tip of Java overlooking the Indian ocean. One of the most beautiful places in Indonesia. Trips to Ujung Kulong can be arranged at Marina Village in Anyer or through the Jakarta booking office (Tel: 323-068).

6. Pelabuhan Ratu

Overnight

Home of Loro Kidul, the Goddess of the South Sea, **Pelabuhan Ratu** is a fishing village on the south coast of Java, famed for its seafood, steep cliffs and wild sea. The **Samudra Beach Hotel** is the focus of a weekend resort which offers nature trails, hot springs, mystical caves and the colourful comings and goings of a traditional fishing community.

It takes about three hours on a good road through spectacular mountain scenery to reach Pelabuhan Ratu from Jakarta. Rent a car or ask at your hotel or a travel agent about coaches. At **Samudra Beach Hotel** you can rent horses to ride on the beach. Fishing boats can be hired at the harbour for a modest fee to skim about on the bay.

Small waterfront restaurants offer excellent fresh seafood and other traditional Indonesian dishes. Hiking trails, nature walks and dramatic coastal scenery add to the rugged, get-away-from-it-all feeling of Pelabuhan Ratu.

Surf and seafood

Dining Experience

Jakarta may have its shortcomings but good food is not one of them. The melting pot nature of the capital is reflected in its cuisine which includes distinct regional cooking from the 27 provinces plus a mixture of other Asian and Western cuisines. There are Indonesian and international restaurants at every budget level; having a good meal should never be a problem and is more often a delight.

A Taste Of Indonesia

"Indonesian cuisine" is a term that really only applies outside the country. Indonesian restaurants in the capital are defined by their regional origin. Fiery Padang cooking from West Sumatra for example, is radically different from the Sundanese cuisine originating from West Java. Even towns have their own speciality dishes and foods; it is a common sight to see travellers, from businessmen on Garuda shuttle flights to village folk on buses, with their luggage in one hand and a woven basket or newspaper parcel of regional delicacies in the other.

There are, of course, common threads that unite the regional cuisines. Rice is the staple of most Indonesian meals, supplemented with chicken, meat, (mutton or goat), fish, vegetables, salads, pickles and the spicy sambal, made from hot chillies. Dairy products are

not used in traditional cooking, fats are derived from coconuts and vegetable oils. As one would expect, cooking in the Spice Islands involves a highly delicate blending of flavours imparted by seeds, roots, leaves, fresh herbs and dried, pounded spices. Although essentially a simple, village, cuisine, Indonesian cooking is sophisticated in taste and highly varied in presentation.

Street Food

The best Indonesian food is still found in the traditional *warung* (roadside stall) and *kaki lima* (vendor cart). Despite the flourishing growth of restaurant business, Indonesians rich and poor continue to patronize these more humble establishments which serve the soul food of the archipelago.

Street food centres are found on **Jl. Asia Africa** (behind the Senayan Stadium), and **Jl. Kendal** (behind the Duku Atas railway station of Jl. Jend. Sudirman). Specialities of the latter include a soup made with your selection of sheep parts (nothing excluded) displayed in large bowls, and Korean barbeque.

Roadside *sate* is found at its best on **Jl. Benhil Raya** (turn left off Jl. Jend. Sudirman just north of the Semanggi flyover) and on **Jl. Sabang**) parallel with Jl. M.H. Thamrin, behind Djakarta Theatre).

Excellent **seafood** and **Chinese dishes** are served after dark on **Jl. Pecenongan** (left off Jl. Juanda in Harmonie). This street is lined with automotive shops by day but in the evening the sidewalks are covered with canvas awnings (usually displaying the house speciality), under which are trestle tables and stools.

For those who wish to savour the delights of street food but are wary of stomach upsets, a marginally more expensive but safer alternative is the restaurant complex in the basement of **Pasaraya** in Blok M. Here the same food as you find on the street is prepared under more hygieneic conditions, with almost every variety of street food and regional cuisine available under one roof.

Dining Indonesian

Tan Goei, opposite the Hero Supermarket on Jl. Cokroaminoto, has indoor and outdoor seating areas, pergolas, fountains and particularly good *sate*. A nice place for a late-night beer and *sate* when the evening breeze is abroad.

Bakmi Gajah Mada in the basement of Studio 21 cinema complex, on Jl. Thamrin and on Jl. Melawai IV in Blok M, do a roaring trade in Indonesian and Chinese noodles cafeteria-style. You get fast service and great noodles.

For HOT and tasty Padang food, **Natrabu** on Jl. Sabang has won prizes for both its cuisine and the waiters' ability to carry 20 or so plates at once. Cheap too.

Senayan Sate House, found on Jl. Cokroaminoto and Jl. Kebon Sirih in Menteng is the best place for inexpensive but delicious *sate* and other excellent Indonesian dishes.

West Java cuisine is found in the various *kuring* restaurants which usually feature indoor gardens and pools from which fresh fish are selected for baking and grilling. Try **Ikan Bakar Kebon Sirih** on Jl. Kebon Sirih or **Raden Kuring** on Jl. Raden Saleh.

Ayam Goreng Mbok Berek is the Indonesian answer to the Colonel, a chain of restaurants specializing in delicious fried chicken.

Stylish Indonesian dining can be enjoyed at **Bengawan Solo**, newly opened in the Sahid Jaya Hotel.

Oasis on Jl. Raden Saleh Raya, housed in a fine Dutch villa, is in a class of its own for old-world style and its traditional *Rijsttafel* served by a long line of waitresses each carrying a separate dish. The food is not outstanding but all who can afford it should visit Oasis for the atmosphere and style.

Indonesian crackers

Dutch/Indonesian

Arts & Curios (Jl. Kebun Binatang, off Cikini II) for good Dutch and Indonesian dishes served in a quaint old curiosity shop atmosphere. Prices are very moderate. A favourite of literary and arty types.

Memories in the Indocement Building on Jl. Sudirman is full of colonial memorabilia and serves good but rich and quite pricey Dutch food.

Dutch food and atmosphere can also be found at **Club Noordwijk**, Jl. Juanda.

Other Cuisines

Japanese

On Jl. Cikini II, just around the corner from Arts & Curios, **Kikugawa** offers some of the most reasonably priced Japanese food and a pleasant atmosphere one might describe as Japanese-rustic.

For excellent *shabu shabu* with panoramic views, **Sky Garden** on the 28th floor of Wisma Nusantara is recommended.

Nippon-Kan in the Hilton is the most pleasant top-of-the-line Japanese restaurant overlooking an ornamental lake with swans and lotus blooms.

Other very good Japanese restaurants are **Shima** in the Hyatt Aryaduta hotel and **Keio** in the Borobudur Intercontinental hotel.

Tokyo Garden in the Lippo Building on Jl. Rasuna Said is also very good, and pricey.

Sumibian (in Chase Plaza on Jl. Jend. Sudirman) specializes in yuppie charcoal *yakiniku*. With views.

Seafood

On Jl. Melawai VIII in Blok M, **Ratu Bahari** serves good Chinese seafood at very moderate prices.

Even better but crowded with connoisseurs at lunchtime is **Nelayan** in Manggala Wanabakti building on Jl. Gatot Subroto.

Nelayan (no relation) in the Borobudur Intercontinental hotel is the best up-market seafood restaurant. The seafood basket, served with pliers and other tools, is very messy but very very good.

Mina Seafood in the Sahid Jaya Hotel is centrally located and has a long-standing reputation for excellent seafood.

Indian

For Indian food, **Orient Express** on Jl. Majapahit and the **George and Dragon** on Jl. Teluk Betung, next door to the Hotel Indonesia are recommended.

A bit further away but worth the journey is **Omar Khayam** on Jl. Antara in Pasar Baru. Erotic murals and real molten silver garnish some dishes.

A different style is offered at **Mutu Curry**, next door to Tanamur disco in Jl. Tanah Abang Timur. Indian rugs, hanging plants and Southern Indian dishes served on banana leaves.

French

The best classic French restaurant in Jakarta is undoubtedly the **Club Room** in the Mandarin hotel. The food is always excellent, the ambience refined and service what you would expect from a first class restaurant.

Running close second are the **Taman Sari** in the Hilton, **Jayakarta Grill** in the Sari Pacific and **Toba Grill** in the Borobudur.

Le Bistro on Jl. Wahid Hasyim is a cosy and popular "French provincial" restaurant and bar, also moderate in price.

An intimate, expensive but elegant French restaurant for romantic trysts is **La Rose** on the ground floor of the Landmark Centre on Jl. Sudirman.

Italian

Jakarta's newest and only up-market Italian restaurant is **Ambiente** in the Hyatt hotel. Elegant interior and excellent service.

An excellent-value buffet lunch and a la carte dinner can be found at the less fancy **Pinocchio** in Wisma Metropolitan I on Jl. Sudirman (with real apes for company), and at **Rugantino** on Jl. Melawai Raya in Blok M.

Despite the balmy tropical nights, there are few places where you can eat out of doors in Jakarta. The Hilton's **Pizzaria**, in the garden behind the hotel, is built out over a lake and features a live band (usually Filipino) every night except Tuesday which is Indonesian Reggae night. Very pleasant and very popular on Friday and Saturday nights.

Pizza Boat in Pondok Indah (nautical decor) also has a very good reputation for pizza.

American/Mexican

The **Ponderosa Family Steakhouses** (Widjojo Centre, Wisma Antara, Centrepoint, Arthaloka Bldg) specialize in steaks and Mexican food with a very good fresh salad bar.

The **Green Pub** in the Jakarta Theatre building on Jl. Thamrin is another good place for Mexican food. Country and western music. Huge margaritas come in a glass you can take home as a trophy.

Green Pub's brother, **Amigos**, in Kemang Club Villas (follow the signs off Jl. Kemang Raya) offers the same successful combination.

Gandy and **Black Angus**, neighbours on Jl. Cokroaminoto, Menteng, are good for western-style steak.

For hamburgers *et al.,* **Bob's Big Boy** in Kuningan Plaza on Jl. Rasuna Said and **Dairy Queen** in Ratu Plaza on Jl. Jend. Sudirman are recommended.

Korean

Koreana on Jl. Melawai VI/3 in Blok M is an unpretentious place offering good Korean food at very reasonable prices.

Also good is **Korea Garden** on Jl. Teluk Betung.

Korea Tower is a more stylish restaurant at the top of the Bank Bumi Daya Building which has a super-fast elevator and spectacular views.

In the medium price range with very good food are the two **Arirang** restaurants on Jl. Gereja Theresia I in Menteng and Jl. Mahakam I in Kebayoran Baru.

Chinese

For medium-priced Szechuan and Cantonese food, try **Summer Palace**, Jl. Menteng Raya 29 and **Hong Kong** on Jl. Blora.

The **Spice Garden** in the Mandarin hotel is an up-market Szechuan restaurant, all red and gold and often full of ostentatiously wealthy patrons. The food and service is superb.

Vietnamese

Paregu on Jl. Sunan Kali Jaya in Kebayoran Baru serves excellent Vietnamese food with piano music and refined service.

Saigon in the Setiabudi Building on Jl. Rasuna Said is also popular.

Shopping

Bargaining is a time-honoured practice in Jakarta. While modern stores have adopted a fixed price policy, in markets and street stalls buyer and vendor defend their own interests. Cautions having been stated, Jakarta offers a wealth of treasures, curiosities and bargains; shopping opportunities are constantly expanding.

What To Buy

Crafts

The people of Indonesia produce a cornucopia of handicrafts. With 27 provinces possessing distinct cultural and artisanic traditions, the range of hand-made goods is phenomenal. The choice of inexpensive gifts to take home includes *batik* clothes, tablecloths etc, *Toraja* coffee in pokerworked bamboo canisters, herbal cosmetics and remedies, wooden kitchen utensils, wooden and leather *wayang* puppets, brassware, leather belts, bags, sandals, jewellery, cushions, alabaster statues, wood carving, basketwork, pottery, shells, filigree silver, precious stones, masks, beadwork, rattan, pewter, East Indonesian *ikats*, Kalimantan weaving and other regional textiles.

Jl. Surabaya, antique shop

Ciputat, antiques

Antiques

Genuine antiques are sold side-by-side with very convincing fakes. The best advice is to buy what you like and can afford; there is nothing wrong with a well-made reproduction. Collectors and serious buyers presumably know their stuff well enough to avoid smooth talking dealers and expensive mistakes.

Furniture

Modern reproduction and old pieces assembled from "spare parts" are now much more common than genuine antiques which fetch international prices. Even so-called "reputable" dealers may lie to you or not know themselves the origin of their goods. If you are buying reproductions, (which are usually well made, look good and won't cost the earth). Choose those made from old wood; unseasoned timber dries out and cracks in non-tropical climates.

Shipping of goods can often be arranged at the time of purchase but make sure you keep copies of all documents and receipts. Shop for antiques such as spice chests, bureaux and marble-topped tables, chairs and bigger pieces including ornately carved Chinese four poster beds.

Brass

Brassware, old and new, is abundant. Genuinely old brassware tends to be of a thicker gauge (heavier) and has a more mellow colour than new brass. Ships' chandlery and colonial lamps are very popular; lamps should be rewired by an electrician at home as they are usually unearthed.

Porcelain

A lot more (convincing) fakes are offered than genuine pieces. A great quantity of Ming porcelain was imported to Indonesia in the early trading era and can still be found for sale. A high price, however, is no indication of real origin. This is an area where you really need to know your stuff if you are spending large sums of money.

Textiles

One of Indonesia's most refined handicraft traditions id the production of ethnic textiles of exquisite beauty and workmanship. Each of the 27 provinces has its own textile art. *Batik* is the most famous, whether the sophisticated and more expensive *batik tulis* (hand-painted), or more common *batik cap* (block printed). Mass produced machine printed *batik* (design on one side of the fabric only) is not the real thing. Another very sophisticated textile is *ikat*, produced by knotting warp threads into elaborate designs before the cloth is dyed. To determine whether a cloth is made with natural (traditional) or synthetic (modern) fibres, hold a thread over a lighted match. Synthetic fibres will melt while natural fibres will burn or smoulder. Antique cloths such as *ikats* or antique and gold leafed *batik* are collectors' items which fetch considerable prices.

Art

Indonesian art is just beginning to find international recognition and some predict that it will come into vogue as with Japanese and Russian art. Some Balinese artists have already established a name and their works are expensive. A handful of modern Indonesian artists are following. Galleries in Jakarta offer a good range of paintings by known artists and talented newcomers. Prices range from very reasonable to very expensive. Old maps and prints of Indonesia mostly come from Europe and are priced accordingly but make a nice souvenir.

Wooden Artifacts

Genuine ethnic woodcarvings are collectors' items and the real McCoy fetches an international gallery price. Most new carvings have been produced for tourists but in the traditional styles of the different tribal regions.

Old pieces tend to be worn smooth in places but new pieces may be artificially aged. *Asmat* wood carving from the far flung region of Irian Jaya is very much in vogue. Carvers in other regions are now copying the *Asmat* style for the tourist market. Genuinely old wooden artifacts are collectors' items, highly sought after by international dealers but still sometimes to be found.

Gold And Silver

Genuine ethnographic jewellery is found in many antique shops but is quite expensive. Modern silver and gold pieces made in traditional designs but with heavier gram weights are a good buy. Well made gold jewellery is a good investment at gold price plus around 10 percent for workmanship. Silver plating used for modern teas sets, spoons etc. is usually thin and tarnishes quickly.

Fashion

Designer fashion is a rapidly developing industry. Prices for off-the-peg garments are very low compared to the West and excellent bargains can be made. Workmanship and fabrics vary a lot so check each item carefully. The best range of Indonesian designer fashions is found in Pasaraya (Blok M), second floor. Leading names include **Ramli, Prajudi, Iwan Tirta, Poppy Dharsono, Arthur Harland, Ghea Sukasah,** and **Hanum Gularso**.

Jamu

Traditional herbal remedies for everything from kidney stones to impotence are sold in little paper envelopes displayed in market stalls and stores. Originally developed by women in the courts of central Java to preserve their beauty and health, *jamu* is now drunk by almost everyone.

Jamu is available in pill form and capsules but the most common is the little packet of powder which is mixed with water to make a drink. The taste is definitely an acquired one but the result is to make one radiant and full of vigour! Many of the *jamu* companies also produce herbal cosmetics, shampoos and tonics made from leaves, spices and natural aromatics which make attractive and unusual gifts.

Where To Buy It

Sarinah department store (Jl. M.H.Thamrin) and **Pasaraya** (Blok M in Kebayoran) carry a huge range of handicrafts that are pretty well representative of everything you can buy in Indonesia, excluding antiques. Because of their bulk buying power, prices are reasonable and quality is consistent.

To save a lot of time and energy when buying take-home gifts, do a one-stop shop at either store, cart all your goods to the wrapping station and write the labels as the man behind the counter wraps. Throw the whole lot in your suitcase and forget about it until you get home.

N.B. For each purchase you will be given a *bon* (bill) which must be taken to the cashier then to a desk where the goods are packaged. Rather than queue to pay each one, collect all the bons as you move around one floor and make one trip to the cashier. Another good one-stop shop is **Keris Gallery**, on Jl. Cokroaminoto in Menteng.

Antique shops are found on **Jl. Pelatehan** in Blok M, good but a bit pricey. The antique and flea market on **Jl. Surabaya** in Menteng is for the more adventurous as bargaining is very much the order of the day.

Many curiosities and genuine antiques, old beads and cloth, china, bric-a-brac and some furniture. If you pay more than half the original asking price you have probably made a bad deal. **Jl. Kebon Sirih Timur Dalam** is a small street in central Jakarta lined with shops full of antiques and furniture. **Jl. Ciputat Raya** is another antique centre about 25 minutes out of town, but prices are cheaper and there is a great selection.

Modern rattan furniture can be found in many shops on **Jl. Kemang Raya**. Check details of workmanship and bargain for at least 15 percent off the asking price. For very reasonably priced batik shop at **Sarinah, Pasaraya, Batik Keris** (Ratu Plaza) and **Danar Hadi** (Jl. Raden Saleh 1A).

Duta Fine Art Foundation is one of the best known art galleries, at Jl. Bangka 1/55A. See artists at work in **Pasar Seni** in the Ancol complex. Paintings and commissioned portraits are for sale. Old prints are available at **Edwins Gallery** on Jl. Kemang Raya 21.

Department Stores

The department store is a rapidly developing entity in Jakarta. **Sogo** is an up-market, Singapore-style store located in the Plaza Indonesia complex. **Mata Hari** in Ratu Plaza, Melawai Plaza and Gajah Mada Plaza have cheap clothes etc. **Robinsons** on Jl. Sabang is handy to Jl. Jaksa and also has a wide range of clothes. **Keris Gallery** is a more fancy store on Jl Cokroaminoto which has a good handicraft section. **Sarinah and Pasaraya** are the best all-round department stores.

Supermarkets

Golden Truly and **Hero** are large all-purpose supermarkets with branches throughout Jakarta. **Kemchicks** (Jl. Kemang Raya) specializes in imported foodstuffs and has very good delicatessen and bread counters.

Markets

The *pasar* is the neighbourhood institution. Although shopping is more efficient in a supermarket (and somtimes cheaper) the pasar is a fascinating place to visit. Bargaining is the order of the day. Every suburb of Jakarta has its own pasar but some specialize in certain types of goods.
Pasar Cikini and **Pasar Minggu** are large all-purposes markets. **Blok M**, **Glodok** and **Pasar Benhil** are good for electronic goods. Harbedashery and textiles, clothes and shoes at **Pasar Tanah Abang** and **Pasar Baru**. **Pasar Ikan** for fish, dried and fresh, ships chandlery, nets, anchors, seashells, stuffed turtles. **Blok A** for ironmongery and household goods, **Pasar Seni** for arts and crafts.

Film Processing

One-hour processing can be done at **Kodak** on Jl. Cokroaminoto, **Fuji** and **Kodak** on Jl. Benhil Raya, **Jakarta Photo** on Jl Sabang. Jakarta Photo is the best all-round photographic store and can do a one-day service for slides. It also does camera repairs and parts. Another camera supply store is located in the first floor of **Ratu Plaza**. Professional slide processing available at **Ekta**, Jl Cideng Barat 80.

Chemist

Prescription drugs can often be bought at the apotik (pharmacy) without a doctor's note. Do not buy medicines from markets as they are sometimes imitations. Large, reliable dispensing pharmacies include **Apotik Senopati** (Jl. Senopati), **Apotik Menteng** (Jl. Dr. Sam Ratulangi) amd **Apotik Melawai** (Jl. Melawai). **Optik Melawai** and **Optik Seis** (many branches) provide eye tests, 24-hour spectacle making, contact lens supplies.

What to Know: Practical Information

TRAVEL ESSENTIALS

When To Visit

Jakarta knows only two types of weather – hot or hot and wet. Residents become attuned to the more subtle variations on these themes but for the traveller, the choice is between a rainy or dry season visit. The rainy season (November to April) is a bit cooler and more pleasant but for sightseeing purposes the dry season (May to October) makes more sense.

Visas

Two-month non-extendable tourist visas are issued to visitors of most nationalities automatically upon arrival through the major ports of entry to Indonesia. (Jakarta, Surabaya, Denpasar, Medan, Manado, Biak, Ambon, Batam, Pekanbaru).

All tourists must have an onward ticket and a passport valid for at least six months. The main immigration office is located on Jl. Teuku Umar 7, Menteng. Open 8 a.m. - 3 p.m. Monday to Thursday; 8 a.m. - 12 noon, Friday; 8 a.m. - 2 p.m., Saturday.

Vaccinations And Health

Vaccination certificates are not required except for travellers coming from areas infected by smallpox, cholera or yellow fever.

Malaria medication is not necessary for a visit to Jakarta but is essential if travelling elsewhere in the country. Gammaglobulin vaccination against hepatitis is also recommended, as are shots for typhoid, paratyphoid and cholera.

Diarrhoea is a common problem for visitors, buy a patent medicine from your chemist at home so you don't have to go looking for one in a strange language when you need it in a hurry.

Money Matters

The sole currency unit in Indonesia is the Rupiah. The Rupiah is inflating slowly but steadily, at the time of writing US$1.00 equals Rp1.870 and this rate can be expected to climb. Banknotes start at 100 rupiah (about US 5 cents) so do not bother to count your coins. The largest banknote is Rp10.000 (around US$5.30) so you have to carry a thick wad of paper. The most useful unit of small change is the Rp1.000 note and a supply of these should be carried in order to avoid the "sorry no change" ploy of taxi drivers and vendors.

Personal cheques even in Rupiah are rarely accepted outside of banks. Credit cards (Amex, Diners, Visa and Mastercard most common) are accepted in nearly all mbig stores, hotels and restaurants and in an increasing number of smaller shops that cater to tourists. Currency other than rupiah is rarely accepted.

Money changers offer slightly better exchange rates than banks and banks slightly better than hotels. Most banks are open 8.30 a.m. to 2 p.m. weekdays and close by midmorning on Saturday.

A small branch of the Bank Pacific, which stays open until 7 p.m. on weekdays and till 5 p.m. on Saturday, is in **Jakarta Hilton Hotel** shopping arcade.

Clothing

Light and loose clothing, preferably in natural or mixed fibres, is recommended. The local women dress modestly, shorts and sleeveless tops are unusual and revealing clothes are considered offensive. Respectable dress should be worn when visiting any government offices.

Footwear should be covered. Open sandals may keep your feet cooler but the filth on Jakarta streets is in a class of its own. Wear rubber thongs (bought anywhere for next to nothing) when you're not wearing shoes to avoid scorpions, worms or the unpleasant sensation of squashing a cockroach barefoot. Uneven Jakarta pavements are hard on shoes and perilous to high heels.

The local all purpose garment, the *sarong*, is immensely practical for both men and women. You can sleep in it, use it as a sheet or pillowcase, shawl, dirty laundry bag (tie up the corners), towel, tablecloth, baby sling, beach cover-up, curtain or wall hanging. Made of cotton *batik*, it folds up to nothing. Wear it in your hotel room without underwear to allow important airing of vital anatomical parts (male and female).

Electricity

Electrical outlets are rated at 220 volts, 50 cycles and take a two rounded pin plug. Extreme caution should be extended when handling all electrical appliances and outlets. On/off switches are rarely provided, appliances and outlets are often unearthed and/or poorly wired. Electrocution and fires caused by short circuits are common. Another reason for wearing rubber thongs.

Airport Tax

A departure tax of Rp9.900 is levied at the airport for international flights. Domestic departures are charged between Rp2.500 and Rp4.000, which is usually but not always included in the ticket price.

GETTING ACQUAINTED

Geography

Indonesia is the world's fifth largest nation (population 187 million) and largest archipelago, composed of more than 17,000 islands stretching for more than 5,000 km (3,100 miles) along the equator.

90 percent of the Indonesian people live on Java, the most densely populated island in the world. More than 8 million live in the capital, Jakarta, which is situated on a swampy alluvial plain on Java's north western coast.

Java is 6 degrees and 17 minutes south of the equator and has a longitude on 106 degrees and 17 minutes east.

The brown Ciliwung river curves through the city along with a network of semi stagnant canals. The city has grown to encompass the fields and plantations that were established on the plain to supply the original trading port. Beyond the plain on all sides, except that facing the sea to the north, rise volcanic hills covered with tea plantations and cooler weather vegetation.

Climate

Temperatures in both wet and dry season are around 27°C (81°F) during the day and slightly lower at night. Humidity is very high, around 81 percent. Heat exhaustion and dehydration can effect visitors not used to the tropics.

Annual rainfall averages close to a metre. During the rainy season expect a truly torrential downpour most days, usually in the afternoon. Expect also to negotiate ankle to knee-deep dirty torrents along streets. Just after the rain, when the air is clean and the streets steam, is a nice time to go out.

Large hotels, restaurants and shops are air-conditioned, in smaller establishments electric fans suffice.

Time

Indonesia is divided into three time zones. Jakarta is on West Indonesia Standard Time, which is GMT plus 7 hours.

How Not To Offend

Jakartans are humorous and easy-going people. There are certain cultural conventions, however, which should be observed. Indonesians are extremely polite and displays of emotion are considered coarse.

It is rude to point with the finger

or foot, to touch anyone on the head, to sit on a table or to use the left hand when giving or receiving money or food. It is customary for men and women to shake hands when meeting. Displays of affection between the sexes are not practised in public; not even holding hands. Members of the same sex may and often do hold hands; this is not a sign of homosexuality. You should say "excuse me" (*maaf*) if you sneeze or blow your nose, you do not need to if you burp.

Most Jakartans are Muslims and do not eat pork or drink alcohol. Drinking, however is generally regarded as a matter of personal choice. Religious and racial tolerance are practised and expected.

Whom Do You Trust?

Indonesians are naturally friendly and nearly always talk to strangers. Being accosted by someone asking questions does not mean he or she is out to dupe you, it's a natural part of social exchange. Having said that, always be on the alert. Violent crime against tourists is extremely rare but petty theft is common. Men should not carry their wallet in a trouser pocket, women should hold a handbag against their body with the opening inwards. As a general rule of thumb, wherever there are crowds, have your hand on your valuables. It is safe for both men and women to walk at night, although common sense should be exercised over dark alleys etc. When in a taxi, check that the meter is switched on, have small change with you to pay the fare and if possible have a rough idea of where you are going to avoid an expensive detour. Lock the doors whenever you are travelling by car. Use hotel safety deposit boxes when they are provided and do not leave luggage unattended anywhere except in a locked hotel room or at a reception desk where a chit is issued.

Tipping

Tipping is common but not absolutely necessary. Where a service charge is added (as in hotels and restaurants) tipping is not necessary. Elsewhere, tip around 5 percent of the bill. Rp500-1.000 is an appropriate tip for porters, room boys, etc. Taxi drivers are not usually tipped beyond keeping the small change from the fare, which they will often do without being asked. Tips will also be sought by various street people offering unwanted services such as wiping the windscreen of your car with a dirty cloth, carrying your bags etc. For reasons of safety they are best ignored.

Tourist Information

Jakarta is not well provided with tourist information. There is a Tourism Office in the Djakarta Theatre building but it has nothing much that cannot be got from a hotel concierge or a travel agent.

Jakarta Program Magazine, avail-

able in most bookstores, gives a monthly listing of what's on in Jakarta, in English. The *Jakarta Post* newspaper (also available in hotels but not at general news stands) gives a daily listing.

GETTING AROUND

Limousines

Usually in the form of Baby Benz or Mercedes Tiger, limousines can be hired from around US$200 per day with petrol and driver. Can be arranged at any five-star hotel.

Taxis

The most sensible way to get around is by taxi unless you are on a very tight budget. Taxis are plentiful and can be flagged down anywhere, fares are cheap by international standards.

Rp5.000 will get you almost any-

where in the city and most journeys can be achieved for less than Rp3.000. There are now many reliable taxi companies but some very dilapidated remnants of Jakarta's infamous former fleet remain. Avoid the really beat-up heaps (usually yellow or green) which are sometimes commandeered by equally unsavoury and unreliable drivers.

Bluebird is the most reputable, long-established taxi company and most drivers speak a bit of English. Bluebird also rent taxis by the hour or day, rate sheets are available from the Bluebird counter at the main door of the Jakarta Hilton hotel.

On Foot

Nobody walks far in Jakarta because of the heat, uncrossable roads, heavy traffic and pollution.

Local Vehicles

Becak, *bajaj* and *bemo* are the three local forms of transport. The *becak* is a pedal powered bicycle with a chair welded on the front. They are prohibited on main roads and unfortunately are being systematically removed from the rest of the city. If you find one, bargain for the fare before you start, most trips should cost Rp300-700.

A *bajaj* is a motorised three-wheeler, usually bright orange in colour, which whizzes in and out of the traffic emitting a lot of noise and fumes. Bargain for the fare before you start, Rp 500-1.000.

A *bemo* is a 7-10 seat mini truck, flagged down anywhere but once again operating mostly off the main roads in the suburbs. The old fashioned *delman* (horse and cart) has almost disappeared from Jakarta but can still be found along Jl. Asia Africa by the Senayan sports complex, in Kebayoran Lama and some other outer suburbs.

Buses

Jakarta buses are very cheap (standard fare Rp200) but are also hot, crowded, dilapidated and frequented by pickpockets who are sometimes in cohorts with the conductor. If you wish to travel by bus, exercise caution. City bus route maps are (sometimes) available from the Jakarta Tourist Information Centre in the Djakarta Theatre building on Jl. Thamrin.

Rental Cars

International firms are expensive, prices start from US$100 per day. Local firms (abundant – ask at any travel agent or hotel) are around 40 percent cheaper. Most of the bigger taxi companies will also rent cars on a daily basis.

An air-conditioned minibus (with or without driver) is good for sightseeing or day trips and works out to be very economical when divided between three or more people.

To And From The Airport

The most expedient way to get into town from Sukarno Hatta (a 30-40 minute journey) is by taxi, fare around Rp20.000 including surcharge and toll fee. There are also air conditioned **Damri** buses (Rp20.000) which serve five city depots with stops on the way.

If you tell the driver your destination, he will usually agree to drop you off at a point nearest to yours along the route.

The buses are much cheaper than a taxi but do not leave until there are sufficient passengers which can mean a considerable wait. Some hotels operate courtesy coaches for guests arriving and departing, check at the hotel reservations counter in the airport terminal. Both buses and taxis are found right outside the terminal doors.

When leaving for Sukarno Hatta, from the city centre, allow 40 minutes in normal traffic conditions and an hour during peak hours 4-7 p.m.

Maps

The most detailed and accurate map of Jakarta is the *Falk Map* available in most bookshops, it is expensive at Rp18.000. Also good (and cheaper) is *Guide & Map of Jakarta*, published by C.V. Pradika and available for Rp4.000 at the Jakarta Hilton bookstall.

Note: House (office, shop) numbers on Jakarta streets often follow no logical sequence, or may follow a sequence for half the street and then go random.

Allow extra time for finding places and if someone gives you an address, always ask for directions as well.

WHERE TO STAY

The hotel industry is just beginning to boom and at the time of writing (November 1990) several new hotels in the three to five-star category are under construction. Booking hotels through a travel agent before you arrive is usually cheaper than walking in off the street. Prices quoted in US$ are for a standard room, single occupancy and do not include tax and service charges.

*****$115-160

Hotel Borobudur Intercontinental
Jl. Lapangan Banteng Selatan
Tel: 370-108
Tlx: 44156 BDOIHC IA
Fax: (62-21) 359-741
(garden, in the city)
$160 night

Mandarin Oriental
Jl. M.H. Thamrin
Tel: 321-307
Tlx: 61755 MANDA IA
Fax: (62-21) 324-669
(city centre)
$150 night

Hyatt Aryaduta
Jl. Prapatan 44-48
Tel: 376-008
Tlx: 46220
Fax: (62-21) 349-836
(city)
$115 night

Sahid Jaya Hotel and Towers
Jl. Jend. Sudirman 86
Tel: 570-4444
Tlx: 46331
Fax: (62-21) 583:168
(city centre)
$124 night

Jakarta Hilton International
Jl. Jend. Gatot Subroto
Tel: 587-981, 583-051
Tlx: JKT 46345 HILTON JAKARTA
Fax: (62-21) 583-091
(garden, city centre)
$135 night

Grand Hyatt Jakarta
Jl M Hm Thamrin
Jakarta 10230
Tel: (21) 335551
Fax: (21) 334321
Tlx: 61534 Hyatt IA
(city cebtre)
$170 night

Le Meridien Jakarta
Jl Jenderal Surdirman Kav
Jakarta 10220
Tel: (21) 588250
Fax: (21) 588252
Tlx: 62960 HOMER IA
(city centre)
&140 night

* * * * $77-125

Hotel Indonesia
Jl. M. H. Thamrin
Tel: 322-008
Tlx: 61233 HTLIND IA
Fax: (62-21)
(city centre)
$100 night

Sari Pan Pacific
Jl. M.H. Thamrin
Tel: 323-707
Tlx: 44514 SARIPA IA
Fax: 323650
(city centre)
$125 night

President
Jl. M.H. Thamrin 59
Tel: 320-508

Tlx: 61401 PREHO IA
Fax: 333631
(city centre)
$80 night

Kartika Chandra
Jl. Gatot Subroto
Tel: 511-008
Tlx: 62474 HKACHA IA
Fax: 5204238
(city)
$77 night

Horison
Jl. Pantai Indah, Ancol
Tel: 680-008
Tlx: 42824 HORIZ JKT
Fax: 684044
(beach)
$78 night

Jayakarta Tower
Jl. Hayam Wuruk 126
Tel: 649-6760
Tlx: 4113JTHJKT IA
Fax: 6295000
(north city)
$60 night

* * * **$32-48**

Kemang
Jl. Kemang Raya
Tel: 793208
(south city)
$56 night

Kartika Plaza
Jl. M.H. Thamrin
Tel: 321-008
(city centre)
$45 night

Wisata International
Jl. M.H. Thamrin
Tel: 320-308
(city centre)
$43 night

Sabang Metropolitan
Jl. H. A. Salim
Tel: 354-031
(city centre)
$48 night

Cikini Sofyan
Jl. Cikini Raya 79
Tel. 320-695
(city)
$37 night

* * **$20-35**

Marco Polo
Jl. Cikditiro, Menteng
Tel: 326-679
(city)
$21 night

Menteng I
Jl. Gondangdia Lama 28
Tel: 325-208
(city)
$30 night

Budget $4-16

The cheapest accommodation in Jakarta is found on **Jl. Jaksa** and neighbouring **Jl. Kebon Sirih Barat Dalam**, in easy walking distance of most downtown amenities. These are the traditional backpacker's haunt; a number of homestays offer simple rooms with fans or, for a little more money, air conditioning. A simple breakfast is often included in the room rate.

The most frequently recommended are **Wisma Delima** at Jl. Jaksa 5, **Borneo Hostel** on Jl. Kebon Sirih barat Dalam 35 and **Bali International** on Jl. K.H. Wahid Hasyim 116.

BUSINESS HOURS

Banks are open from 8.30 a.m. until 1 or 2 p.m., depending on the bank. On Saturday most open from 8.30 a.m. until 11 a.m. but some are closed. Many money changers stay open until 9 p.m. Office hours are generally 8 a.m. until 4 p.m. and people often go home early on Friday. Government offices are open from 8 a.m. until 3 p.m. Monday to Thursday, 8 a.m. until 3 p.m. on Friday and 8 a.m. until 11.30 a.m. on Saturday. Post offices open at 8 a.m. and often close between 1 p.m. and 2.30 p.m. and close again at 4 p.m. Shops open from 9 a.m. until 5 p.m., department stores and large shops stay open until 9 p.m. Most but not all shops are open on Sunday. Restaurants tend to close early by western standards, around 10.30 p.m. or 11.00 p.m. Museums tend to close in the early afternoon and all day Monday.

A simple method which will save frustration is to do all business (bank, post office, tickets etc) and museums in the morning and shopping in the afternoon.

PUBLIC HOLIDAYS

New Year's Day: January 1

Ascension of Mohammed: February 23

Hindu New Year: March 27

Good Friday: April 13

Idul Fitri: April 26-27

Idul Adha: July 3

Hijriah New Year: July 23

Indonesian Independence Day: August 17

Birthday of Prophet Mohammed: October 1

Christmas: December 25

HEALTH AND EMERGENCIES

Health And Hygiene

Diarrhoea often attacks visitors, often due to changes in diet and water, as much as hygiene. On no account drink tap water, anywhere. All drinking water must be boiled. Drinks and ice served anywhere in Jakarta are almost universally made from boiled water - the locals won't drink the stuff neat either. Bottled water, (Aqua or other brand names), is available everywhere including roadside stalls, in small or large bottles and in one-drink sealed plastic cups. First time visitors to the tropics would be wise to carry a small bottle of Aqua around with them - dehydration and heat exhaustion can come over you suddenly and are very unpleasant. Tropical heat can make you feel faint, nauseous, lethargic or all three, until you get used to it. Take it easy, drink as much liquid as possible.

All cuts, scratches and scratched mosquito bites should be disinfected regularly and kept covered to avoid infection. Take the covering off at night to let the wound dry out. Sulphanilamide powder, available from the apotik, is very effective in drawing off moisture. Wounds which stay damp easily turn into tropical ulcers. Use medicated talc (Purol brand available in supermarkets) between legs, toes and under arms to avoid heat rash, crutch rot, athletes foot and other sweaty unpleasantries.

Many prescription medicines can be bought over the counter at *apotiks* (pharmacies). To avoid language confusion, write the name of the medicine you want on a piece of paper and hand it to the person at the counter. Do not buy medicines in markets or from vendors, they may be fakes.

Health Emergencies

Accidents and illnesses: Basically you take your chances. Jakarta has some well-trained medical professionals and good facilities and some that are poorly equipped and slipshod. If you need to get to a hospital in a hurry, call a Bluebird taxi, the ambulance service is not reliable and staff often do not speak English. Most doctors speak some English but hospital staff probably do not. If you go to a hospital you must have enough money with you to pay. Many hospitals will only accept emergencies if they have the space.

The best, most modern hospitals are **Rumah Sakit Pondok Indah**, which also has a 24-hour emergency and ambulance service, and **Pertamina Hospital**, Jl. Kyai Maja, Kebayoran Baru. English speaking doctors are available for home visits at Doctor-on-Call (tel: 683-444/681-405).

Medical Clinics

For less urgent medical care, **SOS Medika** on Jl Prapanca Raya, No.32-34, Kebayoran Baru, is recommended.

(Tel: 733-094/771-578.) Clean and reasonable charges with competent, English speaking doctors. 24-hour emergency service. VD treatment.

Tropical Sex

The legend of the Asian fleshpot lingers on. As yet Jakarta has not contracted AIDS on any scale, but it has a virulent case of everything else. Condoms are readily available in any *apotik* and in many supermarkets and are not considered to be embarrassing items. The word is also condom in Indonesian. Use them.

Dental Clinics

Metropolitan Medical Centre
Jl H.R. Rasuna Said Kav C21
Tel: 520-3433/520-3446

Metropolitan Medical Centre
Wisata International Hotel
Jl M.H. Thamrin
Tel: 320-408

Police Emergencies

The telephone number of the **Jakarta Metropolitan Police** is 510-110. The police headquarters is on Jl. Jend. Sudirman, immediately south of the Semanggi flyover and opposite the Hilton Hotel. Police procedures are rather long-winded and require copious paperwork. Police reports, however, are necessary in the event of lost passports, traveller's cheques etc.

There is a **small police post** in the Sarinah car park on Jl. Thamrin, another on Jl Diponegoro in Menteng.

Emergency Repairs

Shoe repairs (also handbag/luggage/belt repairs) while-you-wait on Jl. Benhil Raya and Jl. Sabang. More expensive but longer-lasting repairs can be found at Sarinah Thamrin, ground floor, three to five days. Tailoring repairs and alterations are quick and cheap in Blok M market, choose any stall with a sewing machine. Camera repairs at Jakarta Photo on Jl. Sabang.

COMMUNICATIONS AND NEWS

Telecommunications And Postal Services

Unlike most cities where post offices are common landmarks, Jakarta post offices are few and far between and not always easy to spot. They also seem to be shut whenever you want to use them. The **main Post Office** at Jl. Pos Utara 2 in the Pasar Baru area, is quite a way from the city centre. It is open 8 a.m.- 4 p.m., Monday to Saturday, but some counters close at 1 p.m. To avoid post office frustration, use the hotel postal counters for all routine mailing.

Outgoing letters take a long time to leave the country, if you can afford it, it is worth paying a little extra for the Express (*Kilat*) service. **Branch offices** which handle most postal services are located in **Sarinah** on Jl. Thamrin (ground floor) and **Jl. Kapten Tendean** in Kebayoran.

Branch offices usually close from 1 p.m. - 2 p.m.

Courier services are another alternative, quicker and safer although considerably more expensive. DHL (Wisma Metropolitan II) is efficient, Usaha Express takes a bit longer but is around half the price. (Counters in Kaliman Travel, President Hotel and at the travel agency on the ground floor of Wisma Metropolitan II).

Public telephones in Jakarta take either Rp50 or Rp100 coins but rarely work. Phones in the hotel lobbies are a better bet. For international calls, the **Telecom Centre** in the Djakarta Theatre building is open 24 hours and is run efficiently.

Shipping

If you are sending packages by mail, do not seal the parcel until you have been to the post office as the contents may have to be inspected.

Shipping companies which regularly handle consignments for foreigners are **Global International**, on Jl. Kemang Raya 20A, Tel. 799-0160 and **Lane Moving & Storage**, Cilandak Industrial Estate, Tel. 7800747.

News Media

The Jakarta Post, *The Indonesia Times* and the *Indonesian Observer* are the three English language daily papers of which *The Jakarta Post* is by far the best. Censorship of local news is fairly standard practice; rules of conduct for the press are laid down by the government with penalties rapidly imposed upon defaulters.

The Jakarta Post, plus imported regional papers like the *Straits Times*, *The International Herald Tribune* and *The Asian Wall Street Journal* are available in hotel book stores.

Jakarta has two TV stations. Indonesian state television, **TVRI**, broadcasts nationwide with some regional programming as well. Apart from the 6.30 evening news, all programs are in Indonesian The second TV channel, RCTI, is a privately owned commercial channel which broadcasts a program in English, only receivable by rented decoders. Most hotels carry both TV channels, along with satellite programs from Malaysia and America. Nearly all radio programs are broadcast in Indonesian. **Radio Republik Indonesia** is the state broadcasting company.

MUSEUMS

National Museum
Jl. Merdeka Barat 12, Ctrl.Jkt
Tel: 360-551

National Monument Museum
Jl. Silang Monas, Ctrl.Jkt
Tel: 340-452

Wayang Museum
Jl. Pintu Besar Utara 27, W.Jkt
Tel: 679-560

Pancasila Sakti Museum
Jl. Pondok Gede Raya, E.Jkt
Tel: 840-0423

Adam Malik Museum
Jl. Diponegoro 29, Ctrl.Jkt

Indonesian Museum
Taman Mini Indonesia Indah
Jl. Pondok Gede Raya, E.Jkt
Tel: 840-0526 ex 383

Soldiers Museum
Taman Mini Indonesia Indah
Tel: 840-1080

Maritime Museum
Jl. Pasar Ikan 1, W.Jkt
Tel: 669-3406

Armed Forces Museum
Jl. Gatot Subroto 147
Tel: 511-795 ex 62

Textile Museum
Jl. K.S. Tubun
Tel: 365-367

Museum Taman Prasasti
Jl. Tanah Abang 1, Ctrl. Jkt
Tel: 377-907

Ethnographic Museum
Jl. Palmerah Selatan 17, S.Jkt
Tel: 548-83008 ex 7233

Philatelic Museum
Taman Mini Indonesia Indah
Tel: 841-310

Forestry Museum
Jl. Gatot Subroto, Ctrl.Jkt
Tel: 584-640 ex 5557

Fine Art Museum
Jl. Taman Fatahillah 1, W.JKt
Tel: 676-090

45 Struggle Museum
Jl. Menteng Raya 31, Ctrl.Jkt
Tel: 356-141

SPORTS FACILITIES

The **Hilton** and **Borobudur** hotels have comprehensive sports facilities with swimming pools, jogging tracks, tennis, squash and fitness centres. The facilities may be used by non-guests on a daily membership basis.

Tennis

Senayan Sports Complex, Jl. Jend. Gatot Subroto, for courts rented on an hourly basis. Also at **Club 25**, Jl Bangka I/25, Mampang.

Jogging

Senayan Sports Complex main arena. **Hilton** and **Borobudur** hotels also have jogging tracks.

Squash

Hotel fitness centres; **Senayan Sports Complex**.

Golf

Kebayoran Golf Club, Jl Asia Africa, Senayan, right in town. **Ancol Golf Course**, Taman Impian Jaya, Ancol, by the sea.

Driving Ranges

The **Kebayoran** and **Ancol** golf clubs have driving ranges, open from early morning until mid-evening.

Scuba Diving

Jakarta Dive School & Pro Shop and **Divemasters**, both in the Hilton Hotel Bazaar, will arrange tuition, weekend and longer diving trips and equipment rental.

The same services are offered by **Stingray Dive Centre** in the Garden Hotel, Kemang, and **Dive Indonesia** in the Borobudur Hotel.

SPECIAL INFORMATION

The Indonesian Language

The Indonesians speak more than 300 dialects, each distinct from, and in many cases unintelligible to the other. To overcome this obstacle to national unity, a single common language, Bahasa Indonesia, was introduced and today it is spoken throughout the archipelago in addition to the local dialects. Bahasa Indonesia is written in Roman script.

Bahasa Indonesia is basically Malay, with some minor variations in spelling and pronounciation. The language also includes a considerable number of words which have come from Portuguese, Dutch, English and Sanskrit. Many words for modern appliances or new concepts have been derived from English but appear in a semi-phonetic form, hence such words as *listrik* (electricity) and *eskrim* (ice cream).

Fortunately grammar is not a major concern when speaking Bahasa Indonesia. Even if you construct a sentence wrongly, it will generally be understood. Any effort to speak the local language is met with enthusiastic encouragement; mistakes are disregarded blithely and there is no need to hang back. Tenses are easily dealt with by using a simple verb with a time indicating word. Hence: I eat (*saya makan*), I already ate (*saya* sudah makan), I haven't eaten yet (saya belum makan) or I'll eat later (nanti saya makan).

Indonesian letters generally represent a single sound, making pronunciation very easy. Vowels: A as in FAR; E as a in AMONG; I as in TIN; O as in DOG; U as in PUT. Double vowels: AI as in LIKE; AU as in COW. Consonants sound the same as in English with the exception of C which sounds like CH as in CHair. Some double consonants appear: KH as in the German iCH; NY as in NEW; SY as in purSUit.

You will sometimes encounter examples of old-style spelling in words such as Djakarta instead of Jakarta, TJ as in Tjandra instead of Candra, OE in Soeharto instead of Suharto. The old spellings are now rarely used, with the exception of OE which is retained only in people's names and only in Indonesia. Thus Soeharto in Indonesia, Suharto in the foreign press.

Courteousness is a feature of the Indonesian language. When addressing others a title of some sort is normally used. *Ibu* or *Nyona* for a married woman, *Nona* for an unmarried woman, *Bapak* or *Mas* for a man. There are several forms of the word YOU which differentiate the status of the speaker and the person spoken to. To make life simpler, a general term, ANDA is now in common use. It is also quite common to speak in the third person when addressing another. Hence Janet to John: Janet: Where is John going? (*John mau kemana?*) John: I'm going to the market, does Janet want to come? (*Ke pasar, Janet mau ikut?*)

Here is some basic vocabulary to get you started.

Numbers

English   Bahasa Indonesia

One	*Satu*
Two	*Dua*
Three	*Tiga*
Four	*Empat*
Five	*Lima*
Six	*Enam*
Seven	*Tujuh*
Eight	*Delapan*
Nine	*Sembilan*
Ten	*Sepuluh*
Eleven	*Sebelas*
Twelve	*Duabelas*
Thirteen	*Tigabelas*
Fourteen to Nineteen	Number + *belas*
Twenty	*Duapuluh*
Thirty	*Tigapuluh*
Forty-Ninety	Number + *puluh*
One Hundred	*Seratus*
One Thousand	*Seribu*
One Million	*Satu Juta*

Greetings And Others

Hello	*Selamat pagi* (morning)
	Selamat siang (11 a.m. – 4 p.m.)
	Selamat sore (afternoon/evening)
	Selamat malam (night)
How are you?	*Apa kabar?*
Well, thank you	*Kabar baik.*
Thank you very much	*Terima kasih banyak.*
May I take a photo?	*Boleh saya foto?*
Never mind	*Tidak apa apa.*
I cannot speak Indonesian.	*Saya tidak bisa bicara Bahasa Indonesia.*
A little.	*Sedikit.*
Where do you live?	*Anda tinggal dimana?*
What is this called in Indonesian?	*Apa namanya ini dalam Bahasa Indonesia?*
How much?	*Berapa?*
I don't understand.	*Saya tidak mengerti.*

Directions And Travel

Where	*Dimana*
Right	*Kanan*
Left	*Kiri*
Turn	*Belok*
Straight ahead	*Terus*
Please slow down	*Pelan pelan*
Stop here	Stop *disini*
Fast	*Cepat*
Hotel	*Hotel*
Street	*Jalan*
Lane	*Gang*
Bridge	*Jembatan*
Police Station	*Pos polisi*

Useful Phrases

Yes	*Ya*
No	*Tidak*
Do you have?	*Ada?*
Expensive	*Mahal*
Do you have something cheaper?	*Ada yang lebih murah?*
Can you lower the price a bit?	*Harganya bisa kurang?*
Do you have another colour?	*Ada warna lain?*
Too big.	*Terlalu besar.*
Too small.	*Terlalu kecil.*
Do you have bigger?	*Ada yang lebih besar?*

Do you have smaller? *Ada yang lebih kecil?*
I don't want it. *Saya tidak mau.*
I want to go to *Saya mau ke*

Other Handy Words

Hot (heat) *Panas*
Hot (spicy) *Pedas*
Cold *Dingin*
Sweet *Manis*
Sour *Asem*
Delicious *Sedap*
Sorry *Ma'af*
Sick *Sakit*

USEFUL ADDRESSES

Foreign Banks

American Express
Arthaloka Building
Jl. Jend. Sudirman 2
Tel: 587-401

Bank of America
Wisma Antara
Jl. Merdeka Selatan 17
Tel: 347-031

Chase Manhattan Bank
Jl. Jend. Sudirman Kav 21
Tel: 578-2213

Citibank
Jl. Jend. Sudirman Kav 70A
Tel: 578-2007

Hong Kong & Shanghai Bank
Wisma Metropolitan II
Jl. Jend. Sudirman
Tel: 578-0075

Embassies

Afghanistan
Jl. Dr. Kusuma Atmaja SH 15
Tel: 333-169

Algeria
Jl. Rasuna Said 10
Tel: 514-719

Argentina
Jl. Panarukan 17
Tel: 338-088

Australia
Jl. M.H. Thamrin 15
Tel: 323-109

Bangladesh
Jl. Mendut 3
Tel: 321-690

Belgium
Jl. Cicurug 4
Tel: 348-719

Brazil
Jl. Teuku Cik Ditiro 39
Tel: 358-378

Britain
Jl. M.H. Thamrin 75
Tel: 330-904

Brunei
Central Plaza, Jl. Jend. Sudirman
Tel: 511-990

Bulgaria
Jl. Imam Bonjol 74
Tel: 343-926

Burma
Jl. H. Agus Salim 109
Tel: 320-440

Cambodia
Jl. Cicurug 6
Tel: 346-836

Canada
Wisma Metropolitan I Fl.5
Jl.Jend. Sudirman
Tel: 510-709

Chile
Jl. H.R. Rasuna Said Kav.10
Tel: 520-1131

China
Jl. Banyumas 4
Tel: 351-212

Czechoslovakia
Jl. Moh. Yamin SH 29
Tel: 310-1068

Denmark
Jl. H.R. Rasuna Said Kav.10
Tel: 520-4350

Egypt
Jl. Teuku Umar 68
Tel: 345-572

Finland
Jl. H.R. Rasuna Said Kav.10
Tel: 516-980

France
Jl. Thamrin 20
Tel: 332-807

Germany
Jl. M.H Thamrin 1
Tel: 323-908

Greece
Jl. Kebon Sirih 16
Tel: 347-016

Hungary
Jl. H.R. Rasuna Said Kav.X/3
Tel: 587-521

India
Jl. H.R. Rasuna Said 51
Tel: 520-4150

Iran
Jl. HOS Cokroaminoto 110
Tel: 331-378

Iraq
Jl. Teuku Umar 38 Pav
Tel: 344-557

Italy
Jl. Diponegoro 45
Tel: 337-422

Japan
Jl. M.H Thamrin 24
Tel: 324-308

Korea (North)
Jl. Jend.Gatot Subroto Kav.57
Tel: 512-509

Korea (South)
Jl. Teuku Umar 72-74
Tel: 332-846

Malaysia
Jl. Imam Bonjol 17
Tel: 332-664

Mexico
Jl. M.H Thamrin 59
Tel: 337-974

Netherlands
Jl. Rasuna Said Kav. S.3
Tel: 511-515

New Zealand
Jl. Diponegoro 41
Tel: 330-680

Nigeria
Jl. Diponegoro 34
Tel: 327-838

Norway
Jl. H.R Rasuna Said Kav.10
Tel: 510-638

Pakistan
Jl. Teuku Umar 50
Tel: 346-523

Panama
Speed Building
Jl. Gajah Mada
Tel: 341-995

Papua New Guinea
Wisma Metropolitan Fl. 4
Jl. Jend. Sudirman Kav 29
Tel: 584-604

Philippines
Jl. Imam Bonjol 6-8
Tel: 310-0302

Poland
Jl. Diponegoro 65
Tel: 320-509

Portugal
Wisma Nusantara
Jl. M.H.Thamrin
Tel: 356-111

Romania
Jl. Cikditiro 24 A
Tel: 349-524

Saudi Arabia
Jl. Imam Bonjol 13
Tel: 359-838

Singapore
Jl. H.R Rasuna Said Bl X/4 Kav. 4
Tel: 520-1469

Spain
Jl. M.H Thamrin 53
Tel: 325-996

Sri Lanka
Jl. Diponegoro 70
Tel: 321-018

Sweden
Jl. H.R Rasuna Said Kav.10
Tel: 520-1551

Switzerland
Jl. H.R Rasuna Said Bl/X3 Persil 2
Tel: 516-061

Syria
Jl. Diponegoro 21
Tel: 324-240

Thailand
Jl. Imam Bonjol 34
Tel: 343-762

Turkey
Jl. Imam Bonjol 43
Tel: 349-500

United States Of America
Jl. Medan Merdeka Selatan 4-5
Tel: 360-360

USSR
Jl. Imam Bonjol 60
Tel: 346-423

Vatican Kingdom
Jl. Merdeka Timur 17
Tel: 341-142

Yemen
Jl. Gondangdia Lama 37A
Tel: 345-225

Airline Offices

Air India
Hotel Sari Pacific
Jl. Thamrin.
Tel: 325-534

Air Canada
Hotel Sabang Metropolitan
Jl. H.A.Salim
Tel: 371-479

British Airways
Wisma Metropolitan I
Jl. Sudirman
Tel: 578-2460

Cathay Pacific
Hotel Borobudur
Jl. Lapangan Banteng
Tel: 380-6664

China Airlines
Duta Merlin
Jl. Gajah Mada
Tel: 354-448

Czechoslovak Airlines
Wisata International Hotel
Jl. Thamrin
Tel: 325-530

Garuda Indonesia
Wisma Dharmala Sakti
Jl. Jend. Sudirman 32
Tel: 588-707

Japan Airlines
Wisma Nusantara, Jl. Thamrin
Tel: 322-207

KLM
Plaza Indonesia, Jl. Thamrin
Tel: 320-708

Korean Air
Wisma Metropolitan II
Jl. Sudirman
Tel: 578-0236

Lufthansa
Panin Centre
Jl. Sudirman
Tel: 710-247

Malaysian Airlines System
Hotel Indonesia
Jl. Thamrin
Tel: 320-909

Northwest Orient
Wisma Bumiputera
Jl. Sudirman
Tel: 520-3152

Saudi Arabian Airlines
Wisma Bumiputera
Jl. Sudirman
Tel: 578-0615

Singapore Airlines
Chase Bldg.
Jl. Sudirman
Tel: 584-011

Swissair
Hotel Borobudur
Jl. Lapangan Banteng
Tel: 373-608

Thai International
BDN Bldg.
Jl. Thamrin
Tel: 320-607

Trans World Airlines
Wisma Bumiputera
Jl. Sudirman
Tel: 578-2145

United Airlines
Hotel Borobudur
Jl. Lapangan Banteng
Tel: 362-707

UTA
Jaya Bldg.
Jl. Thamrin
Tel: 323-609

Pan Am
Hotel Borobudur
Jl. Lapangan Banteng
Tel: 361-707

Philippine Airlines
Hotel borobudur
Jl. Lapangan Banteng
Tel: 370-108

Qantas
BDN Bldg.
Jl. Thamrin
Tel: 327-707

Republic Airlines
Wisma Metropolitan II
Jl. Sudirman
Tel: 578-1710

Royal Brunei Airlines
Hotel Sabang Metropolitan
Jl. H.A. Salim
Tel: 376-237

Sabena Airlines
Hotel borobudur
Jl. Lapangan Banteng
Tel: 370-108

Cultural Centres

Australian Cultural Centre
Bank Niaga Bldg.
Jl. M.H. Thamrin 55
Tel: 330-453

The British Council
Widjojo Centre
Jl. Jend. Sudirman 56
Tel: 587-411

French Cultural Centre
Jl. Salemba Raya 25
Tel: 882-284

Erasmus Huis (Dutch)
Jl. H.R. Rasuna Said
Tel: 512-321

Goethe Institute (German)
Jl. Matraman Raya 23
Tel: 884-139

Indonesia-America Friendship Society
Jl. Pramuka Kav 30
Tel: 881-241

Italian Cultural Centre
Jl. Diponegoro 45
Tel: 340-964

Japan Cultural Centre
Jl. Cemara 1
Tel: 367-409

Churches

Churches which conduct services in English:

All Saints Church (Anglican)
Jl. Arif Rahman Hakim 5, Menteng
Tel: 345-508

St Cansius College Chapel
(Roman Catholic)
Jl. Menteng Raya 64, Menteng
Tel: 325-546

Gereja Emanuel (Protestant)
Jl. Medan Merdeka Timur 10, Jakarta Pusat

American Southern Baptist
Jl. Tirtayasa Raya 1, Kebayoran Baru
Tel: 799-1062

First Church of Christ Scientist
Jl. Tengku Cikditiro 48, Menteng
Tel: 351-962

Church of Jesus Christ of the Latter Day Saints (Mormon)
Jl. Dr Saharjo 317B, Tebet
Tel: 829-8390

Church of Christ
Jl. Sumatera 19, Menteng
Tel: 768-196

Charismatic Worship
Jl. Senen Raya 6, Senen
Tel: 343-200

FURTHER READING

Books on Indonesia, in English and other languages, are readily obtainable in hotel bookstands in the **Hyatt**, the **Borobudur** and **Sari Pacific**. Also well-stocked is the **Arthaloka News stand** in the Arthaloka Building on Jl. Sudirman. **Times** bookstore and **Indra International** bookstore have many English titles and are found in Wisma Dharmala Sakti, also on Jl. Sudirman.

Jakarta

Zach, Paul & Edleson, Mary Jane. *Jakarta*. Times Travel Library. Times Editions, Singapore, 1987.
A good general introduction to the city, well illustrated.

American Women's Association. *Jakarta Shopper's Guide*. AWA, Jakarta 1987.
By expats for expats. Very practical information on where to get what.

General

American Women's Association. *Introducing Indonesia*. AWA, Jakarta, 1988.
Concise and extremely practical handbook for living in Jakarta.

Dalton, Bill. *Indonesia Handbook*. Moon Publications, Chicago, 1985.
Classic hippie travel guide, still a favourite.

Hutton, Peter. *Insight Guide: Java*. Apa Publications

History

Heuken, Adolf, S.J. *Historical Sites of Jakarta*. Yaysan Cipta Loka Caraka, 1982.
Engaging and detailed account of Jakarta's historic landmarks.

McDonald, Hamish. *Suharto's Indonesia*. University Press of Hawaii, 1980.
Helpful background to the current regime.

Ricklefs, M.C. *A History of Modern Indonesia*. Macmillan Press Ltd, London, 1985.
Authoritative textbook.

Thomson Zainu'ddin, Ailsa G. *A Short History of Indonesia*. Cassell Australia Ltd, Stanmore, 1980.
A good textbook by an Islamic scholar.

Religion

Edmonds, I.G. *Islam*. Watts, 1977.

Edmonds, I.G. *Islam.* Watts, 1977.

Epton, Nina. *Magic & Mystics of Java.* Octagon Press, London, 1974.

Arts And Culture

Alisjahbana, Sutan Takdir. *Indonesia: Social and Cultural Revolution.* Oxford University Press, 1966.
A collection of essays, quite often critical.

Draine, Cathie & Hall, Barbara. *Culture Shock: Indonesia.*
A very practical guide to understanding the social graces and mores of the Indonesian people.

Elliot, Inger McCabe. *Batik: Fabled Cloth of Java.* Clarkson N. Potter, Inc. 1984.

Holt, Claire. *Art in Indonesia: Continuities and Change.* Cornell University Press, New York, 1967.
Considered a modern classic. Research on the arts conducted while travelling in Java and Bali.

Pucci, Idanna. *The Epic of Life.* Alfred van der Marck Editions, 1985.

Tirtaamidjayaja, N. *Batik: Pattern and Motif.* Djambatan 1966,

ART/PHOTO CREDITS

Photography	**Ingo Jezierski**
Maps	**Berndtson & Berndtson**
Cover Design	**Klaus Geisler**

Index

A

Adam Malik, 31, 51
Adam Malik Museum, 89
adat (codes of customs), 17
Agung Mosque, 60
Ambassador Lounge, 31, 55
Ambiente (Italian restaurant), 69
Amigos (pub), 55, 70
"Amsterdam of the East" (Batavia), 20
Anak Krakatau (son of Krakatau), 62
Ancol (village), 42
Ancol Marina, 43, 59
Andries Hartsinck, 45
angklung (instrument composed of hollow bamboo), 17, 27
antique flea market, 31, 43
Apotik Jawa, 40
Apotik Menteng (chemist), 77
Apotik Senopati (chemist), 77
Apung Restaurant, 43
antiques, 53, 72, 76
Anyer resort, 63
architecture, 16
Arirang restaurant, 70
Arjuna, statue of Hindu hero, 23
Armed Forces Museum, 89
Asmat wood carving, 74
Art and Culture, 16, 99
"Art & Curio", 27, 67, 73
Arthaloka Building, 69
"Art of the Tropical Nap", The, 22
Artifacts, 74
ayam goreng (fried chicken), 44
Ayam Goreng Mbok Berek, 66

B

Bali Island (Jetset playground), 4
baked fish (ikan bakar), 25, 44
Bangka Tin, 50
Bakmi Gajah Mada restaurant, 66
Bank Bumi Daya Building, 70
Bank Rakyat Indonesia, 49
Banten (Muslim Javanese Kingdom), 12, 20, 60
Batavia, 13
Batavia City, 12, 13, 20, 24, 28
batik Berdikari factory, 45
batik factory, 44
Batik Hajadi (batik shop), 47
Batik Keris shop (Ratu Plaza), 76
batik tulis cloth (handdrawn cloth), 26, 45, 73
Bharata Theatre, 54
Bengawan Solo Restaurant, 66
Bintang beer, 43
bird market, 48, 51, 52
Bird Park, 41
Black Angus Restaurant, 70
Block M, 49, 56, 66, 69, 70, 76
Bluebird taxi, 32
Blue Ocean club, 55
Bob's Big Boy Restaurant, 70
Bogor Brasserie Restaurant, 56
Bogor town, 34
Bogor Botanical Gardens, 32
Bon Vita Health Massage, 49
Borobudur Intercontinental Hotel, 53, 55, 56
Botanical Gardens, 59
Brass, 72
bubur ayam (chicken porridge), 23, 56
Budi Utomo, 20
Bugis people, 28

C

cable car, 41
Camphuis, Governor General, 95
Captain's Bar, 55
Carita Beach, 60, 62
Catholic Cathedral, 53
Chicago Entertainment Club 56
Chic Mart, 38
Chinatown, 15, 20, 42
Chinese dishes/seafood, 65
Chulalongkorn (King of Thailand), 24
Churches, see list, 97, 98
Ciliwung River, 12
Cipanas village, 59
Ciputat village, 43, 44
Circlek store, 38
Club (bar), 56
Club Noordwijk, 67
Club Room Restaurant (French Food), 68
Coen, Jan Pieterzoon (Dutch envoy), 12, 30, 59
Courtesy, 80, 81
Cuisines
    American/Mexican Food, 69
    Chinese, 70
    French, 68
    Indian, 68

Indonesian, 64, 65
Italian, 69
Japanese, 67
Korean, 70
Seafood, 67
Vietnamese, 70
Culemborg bastion, 28
crafts, 71, 74
Cultural Centres, *see* list, 97
Currencies, *see* 78, 79

D

Dairy Queen Restaurant, 70
Danar Hadi (batik shop), 76
Dandaels, Herman William, 13, 20, 53
Declaration of Independence 1945, 20
Demak (Muslim Javanese Kingdom), 12
Dhamelier (French artist), 37
DHL Courier Service, 88
Diamonds and Lopidaries, 38
Diponegoro (Javanese warrior prince), 24
Dirgantara Pub, 56
Discussion (feature of Indonesian life), 17
Djakarta Theatre building, 26
Dolphin Shows, 42
Dragons in Paradise, 32
Duku Atas railway station, 65
Dunia Fantasy (fun park), 43
Duta Fine Arts Foundation, 37, 76
Dutch education, 13
Dutch East India Company (VOC), 12, 20
Duta Gallery, 37
Dutch traders, 20

E

Ebony entertainment, 56
es campur (fruit drink), 49
Edwin's Gallery, 37, 38, 76
Ekta (shop, slide processing), 77
Es Kelapa Muda (iced young-coconut juice), 25, 44
Electricity, 79
Ethnographic Museum, 89

F

fashion, 75
Fatahillah, (Muslim Prince), 20
Fine Art, 36
Fine Art Museum, 31, 51, 89
fish tanks, 48
flower market, 48
Food, 65-68
Forestry Museum, 89
Fort Speelwijk, 60
Frans Tambuan (film star), 56
fruit stalls, 48
Fuji (photo shop), 77
furniture, 72

G

Galactica (bar/restaurant), 55
Gajah Mada Plaza, 76
gamelan (music of Java), 17, 54
Ganesha society, 24
Gang Gang Sullai (Korean Restaurant), 38
Gedung Tinggi (high house), 45
Geography, 80
George and Dragon Restaurant, 68
Ghea Sukasah (fashion designer), 75
Global International (shipping), 88
Glodok market, 77
Gold and Silver, 74
Golden Snail building, 40
gold stores, 50
Golden Truly Supermarket, 77
gong factory, 34
gotong royong (policy of mutual assistance), 18
Grandy Restaurant, 70
Green Pub (for Mexican food), 55, 69
Gujarat (region in India), 18
Gunung Gede volcano, 59

H, I

Hadiprana Galleries, 50
Haji, (title received after visited Mecca), 18
Hall of Justice, 31
Handicrafts, 16, 26, 49, 51, 71
Hani and Roberts Village, 39
Hanumn Gularso (fashion designer), 75
Harland, Arthur (fashion designer), 75
Health and Emergencies, 86, 87
Hero Supermarket, 39, 43, 66, 77
H & R Village, 39, 40
Hilton Hotel, 32, 44, 54, 56, 79
historic graveyard, 44
Hong Kong (Chinese Restaurant), 70
Hong Kong Bank building, 31
Horison Hotel, 42
Hotel Borobudur, 53
Hotel Indonesia, 3, 23, 34, 55
Hotel Indonesia roundabout, 15, 40, 51, 53
Hyatt Aryaduta hotel, 31, 55, 69
ikan bakar, (baked fish), 25
Ikan Bakar Kebon Sirih (food), 66
Indonesian Communist Party, 20
"Indonesian cuisine", 64, 65
Indonesia Indah, film, 41
Indonesian Language, 90-93
Indonesian Museum, 89
Indonesian Reggae night, 69
Irian Jaya (New Guinea), 53
Islam, 17
Islam Law (the Five Pillars or rituals), 18
Istana Cipanos, 59
Istana Negara (or State Palace), 24
Istiqlal Mosque, 25
Iwan Tirta Shop, 39
Iwan Tirta (fashion designer), 39, 75

J

Jalan (road),
Jl. Agus Salim road, 26, 39
Jl. Asia Africa, 65
Jl. Bangka I road, 36, 37
Jl. Bangka Selatan road, 38
Jl. Barito road, 48
Jl. Basuki road, 40
Jl. Benhill Raya road, 65, 77
Jl. Berdikari Mesjid Al Dawah road, 45
Jl. Budi Kemulyaan road, 23
Jl. Cikditiro road, 28
Jl. Cikini II road, 27
Jl. Cikini Raya road, 27, 54
Jl. Ciputat Raya road, 43, 76
Jl. Cokroaminoto, 70
Jl. Diponegoro road, 51, 52
Jl. Dr. Sam Ratulangi road, 77
Jl. Duren Bangka road, 37
Jl. Empang road, 34
Jl. Gereja Theresia, 70
Jl. Hayam Wuruk road, 31, 55
Jl. H.O.S. Cokroaminoto road, 39, 66, 76
Jl. Iman Bonjol road, 39, 51
Jl. Jendral Sudirman road, 14, 15, 23, 55, 65, 70
Jl. Juanda road, 34
Jl. Kebayoran Lama road, 45
Jl. Kebun Binatang road, 27, 67
Jl. Kebun Sirih road, 27, 66
Jl. Kebun Sirih Timur Dalam road, 53, 76
Jl. Kemang Raya road, 37, 38, 70, 76
Jl. Kendal road, 56, 65
Jl. Kyai Maja road, 48
Jl. Lapangan Banteng Selatan road, 53
Jl. Medan Merdeka Barat road, 23, 24
Jl. Medan Merdeka Utara road, 24
Jl. Melawai road, 72
Jl. Melawai VIII road, 50
Jl. M.H. Thamrin, 14, 15, 23, 76
Jl. Mesjid Palmerah VII road, 45
Jl. Otto Iskandardinata road, 34
Jl. Pakin road, 28, 29
Jl. Palmerah Barat road, 45
Jl. Palmerah Utara road, 47
Jl. Pancasan road, 34
Jl. Pasar Ikan (fish market) road, 28, 29
Jl. Pecenongan road, 65
Jl. Pegangsaan Timur road, 51
Jl. Pekalongan road, 39
Jl. Pintu Utara road, 30
Jl. Prapatan road, 31
Jl. Proklamasi road, 53
Jl. Pulo road, 34
Jl. Raden Saleh road, 31
Jl. Sabang road, 22
Jl. Salemba Raya, 52
Jl. Satsuit Tuban road, 47
Jl. Surabaya road, 28, 31
Jl. Sultan Hasanuddin, 49, 50
Jl. Surya Kencana road, 34
Jl. Tanah Abang Timur road, 47, 56
Jl. Warung Buncit Raya road, 37

Jl. Wolter Monginsidi road, 49
Jaya Ancol Dreamland complex, 55
Jaya Pub, 56
Jayakarta (old name Batavia), 12, 15
Jakarta Bay, 42, 59
Jayakarta Grill, 68
Jakarta Handicraft Centre, **39**
Jakarta History Museum, 30
Jakarta Photo, 77
Jakarta Theatre building, 69
Jakarta Program (guide book), 3
jamu (Indonesian herbal remedies), 51, 75
Japanese invade Batavia (1942), 13, 20
jewellery, 38
Jepara town, 16
Juice 88 (pub), 48

K

Kaaba (secret black stone), 18
K Bar, 56
Kampongs, (villages), 36
Kartini Basuki (Indonesian artist), 37
Kebayoran Baru town, 14, 15, 56
Kebun Raya (botanical garden), 33
Keio (Japanese restaurant), 67
Kemang suburb 36
Kemang Club Villas complex, 55
Kemchicks supermarket, 77
Kemang Club Villas, 70
Kemayoran airport, 61
Keong Mas building, 41
Kikugawa (Japanese food) 67
King's Head (pub), 56
Kodak (photo shop), 77
Kolam Renang Cake, 44
Komodo dragon, 34
Komodo & Ragunan Zoo, 32
Koningsplein (Medan Merdeka), 13, 24
Kon Tiki Bar, 55
Koran (Islam holy book), 18
Koreana (Korean restaurant), 70
Korea Gordon (eating house), 70
Korea Tower Restaurant, 70
Kretek, (clove perfumed cigarette), 15
Krakatau volcano, 60, 62
Krakatau Beach Hotel, 62
kris (wavy-bladed dagger), 16
Keris Gallery, 40, 76, 77
Kudus town, 16
Kudus Bar, 55
Kuningan town, 14
Kuningan Plaza, 70

L, M

Lane Moving & Storage (shipping), 88
La Rose Restaurant, 68
Le Bistro (French restaurant), 68
Loro Kidul (Goddess of The South Sea), 63
Lapangan Banteng (deer field), 53
Landmarks, 14

Lubang Buaya (crocodile hole), 14
Mahkamah Agung (Supreme Court), 53
Majapahit Art & Curio, 50
Mandarin Oriental Hotel, 55
Manggala Wanabakti building, 68
Marco Polo hotel, 28
Mata Hari Departmental Store, 76
Mataram (kingdom), 20
Marina Village, 63
Maritime Museum, 89
Maughamesque beverage, 31
Mecca (holy city of Islam),
Medan Merdeka (park), 24
Melati Lounge, 27, 55
Memories Restaurant, 67
Menteng town, 28, 31, 38, 39, 54, 70, 76
Menteng Plaza, 39
Merdeka Palace, 21
Merdeka Square, 15
Melawai Plaza, 76
Metropolitan Medical Centres, 87
Migrants, 15
Mina Seafood Restaurant, 68
Ministry of Finance, 53
Mohammed Hatta (ex-Vice President), 52
Mohammed (prophet of Islam), 18
Museum Bahari (Maritime Museum), 29
Museum Taman Prasasti, 89
musholla (small mosque), 36
Music Room (disco), 56
Mutu Curry Indian Restaurant, 47, 68

N, O

Natrabu Restaurant, 66
nasi campur (meal on one plate), 43
National Monument Museum, 89
National Monument (Monas), 3, 13, 15, 22, 24, 25, 89
Nelayan Seafood Restaurant, 68
News Media, 88, 89
New Order government, 14, 21
Nippon-Kan Japanese Restaurant, 67
Nirwana Super Club, 55
noodles with Chicken and Soup (bakmi ayam pangsit), 34
Nusantara Building, 34
Oasis Restaurant, 31, 66
Oceanarium, 42
old City Wall, 29
Omar Khayyam Restaurant, 68
Optik Melawai (optician) 77
Optik Seis (optician), 77
Orang Betawi, 11, 15
Oriental disco, 56
Orient Express (Indian food) Restaurant, 68
Oud Gondangdia (street name), 39

P

Padang Restaurant, 26
Paneasila (the state ideology), 17
Pancasila Sakti Museum), 89
Paregu Restaurant (Vietnamese Food), 70
Parrots (bar/restaurant), 55
Pasar Burung (bird market), 48, 51, 52
Pasaraya,, 49, 66, 75, 76, 77
Pasar Baru (market), 77
Pasar Benhil (market), 77
Pasar Cikini, 51, 77
Pasar Ikan (fish market), 77
Pasar Minggu (market), 77
Pasar Tanah Abang (market), 77
Pasar Seni, 42, 55, 76, 77
Patai Nasional Indonesia (PNI), 20
Peacock Cafe, 44
Peacock Coffee Shop, 56
Pelabuhan Ratu (fishing village), 63
Pendopo Bar/Lounge, 53, 55
People, 4, 10, 11, 15, 17, 28
Perkutut (Java Turtle dove), 52
Pertamina Hospital, 87
Pete's Tavern, 56
Philatelic Museum, 89
photographic stores, 50
pinisi sailing boat, 28
Pinocchio Restaurant, 69
Pitstop disco, 56
Pizza Boat Restaurant, 69
Pizzaria (bar), 55, 69
Planters Punch (drink), 31
Plaza Indonesia, 23, 76
President Hotel, 34
Ponderosa Family Steakhouses, 69
Pondok Indah, 69
Porcelain, 72
Prajudi (fashion designer), 75
Poppy Dharsono (fashion designer), 75
Portuguese bronze cannon (Si Jagur), 30
Portuguese spice merchant, 12
Pro Art, 38
Prinsenpark (street name), 39
Pulau Bidadari (resort island,) 59
Pulau Damarb (island), 59
Pulau Kahyangan (island), 59
Pulau Onrust (island), 59
Pulau Kelor (island), 59
Pulau Pelangi, 61
Pulau Putri (island), 61
Pulau Seribu (thousand islands), 61
Puncak Pass, 56
Puncak Pass Hotel, 59
Putri Pulau Seribu Paradise, 61

R

Raden Kuring (food), 66
Raffles, Olivia Mariamme (Raffles' wife), 33, 47
Raffles, Thomas Stamford, 20, 33, 47
Ragunan Zoo, 34

Ramadhan (fasting month), 18
Ramayana Terrace, 23, 56
Ramli (fashion designer), 75
Rattan House, 38
Ratu Bahari Restaurant, 67
Ratu Plaza, 70, 76, 77
Religion, 17
Residence of U.S. Ambassador, 40
Restaurant Fatahillah, 30
Rijsttaffel, 31
Rima Melati (film star), 56
Robinsons (departmental store), 76
Rugantino Restaurant, 69
Rumah Sakit Pondok Indah (hospital), 87

S

Safari Park, 58
Saigon Restaurant, 70
Samudra Beach Hotel, 63
Sari Kuring Restaurant, 25
Sari Pacific hotel, 27, 56, 58
Sarinah (department store), 23, 25, 76, 77
Sate (barbecue meat), 65
Sayur Asem (tamarind soup), 44
Schouwberg Playhouse, 54
Scuba Diving, 90
Senayan Stadium, 65
Shima (Japanese restaurant), 67
Shipping, 88
Shopping Arcade, 53
Siam Garden (Thai Restaurant), 31
Si Jagur (Portugese bronze cannon), 30
Situ Gintung village, 44
Silver plating, 74
Skull of the Java Man, 24
Sky Garden Restaurant, 34, 67
Sogo (department Store), 76, 77
Soldiers Museum, 89
Sop buntut (oxtail soup), 56
SOS Medika (medical clinic), 87
South Sulawesi, 28
Soy bean cakes (tempe), 26
Specx, Jacques (Coen's successor), 12
Spice Garden (Szechuan restaurant), 70
Sriwedari Garden restaurant, 32
Stadhuis (old city hall), 30
Stardust cinema, 56
45 Struggle Museum, 89
Studio 21 Cinema Complex, 66
Sudanese restaurant, 25
Suharto, General, President, 14, 20, 21, 33
Sukarno (ex-President), 13, 14, 20, 52
Sumibian Restaurant, 67
Summer Palace (Chinese Restaurant), 70
Sunda Straits, 62, 63
Sundowners bar, 56

Sumatran tigers, 34
Sunda Kelapa seaport, 3, 12, 20, 28, 60
Supreme Court (Mahkamah Agung), 53
Surosowan Palace, 60

T

Taman Fatahillah (city square), 28, 29
Taman Ismail Marzuki road, 54
Taman Mini Indonesia Indah, 40
Taman Prasasti Cemetery, 47
Taman Proklamasi (Proclamation Park), 52
Taman Sari Restaurant, 68
Taman Suropati, 40
Tambora bar, 56
Tanah Abang market, 47
Tanamur nightspot, 47, 56
Tan Ek Tjaon Bakery and Restaurant, 34
Tan Goei Restaurant, 40, 66
Tanjung Priok harbour, 61
Tavern, the, 55
tempe (soy bean cakes), 26
Temptation (bar/restaurant), 55
Textiles, 16, 45, 47, 73, 89
Textile Museum, 47, 89
Tokyo Garden (Japanese Restaurant), 67
Topaz (bar/restaurant), 55
Top Gun (entertainment), 56
Toraja coffee, 26
Tourist Information, 81, 82
Tropical Sex, 87

U – Z

Uitkijk Tower, 28, 29
Ujung Kulong (nature reserve), 63
Usaha Express (courier service), 88
Van Imhoff, Baron Gustaf Willem, 33
VOC, (Dutch East India Company), 12, 20
Wan De Yuan Temple, 60
warung (roadside stall), 65
wayang (traditional theatre), 17, 54
   wayang golek (puppets show)
   wayang kulit (shadow puppets)
   wayang orang (performed by human)
Wayang Museum, 30, 89
Welcome Monument, 15, 23
Wisma Antara, 69
Wisma Argo Menunggal, 56
Wisma Hayam Wuruk, 31
Wisma Metropolitan, 55, 69
Wisma Nusantara, 67
Wooden Artifacts, 74
Year of Living Dangerously (film), 3
Zoological Musem, 34